Hedda Gabler

Ibsen wrote *Hedda Gabler* in Munich in 1890, shortly before his return to Norway after twenty-seven years of self-imposed exile. The play was intended as a tragedy of the purposelessness of life and in particular of the purposelessness imposed on the women of his time, both by their upbringing and by the social conventions which limited their activities. In 1891 it was produced in Munich, Berlin, Stockholm, Gothenburg, Copenhagen, Christiania and London. Everywhere it met with misunderstanding and abuse. It has nevertheless become one of the most popular of Ibsen's plays and has been professionally staged no less than seventeen times

Michael Meyer's translation was first performed at the 4th Street Theatre, New York in 1960. It was performed by the National Theatre Company at the Old Vic in 1970.

'Meyer's translations of Ibsen are a major fact in one's general sense of post-war drama. The feat is one of profound imaginative sympathy and re-creative freedom. Their vital pace, their unforced insistence on the poetic centre of Ibsen's genius, have beaten academic versions from the field. Meyer has restored to Ibsen's texts the electric "strangeness" which shocked and ultimately mastered 19th century feeling.'

George Steiner in the New Statesman

The photograph on the front cover shows Maggie Smith as Hedda and John Moffat as Judge Brack in the 1970 National Theatre production and is reproduced by courtesy of Zoe Dominic. The photograph on the back cover is reproduced by courtesy of the Mansell Collection.

Methuen's Theatre Classics

Henrik Ibsen

HEDDA GABLER

Translated from the Norwegian by
MICHAEL MEYER

EYRE METHUEN
LONDON

First published in Great Britain by
Rupert Hart-Davis Ltd 1962
© *Michael Meyer 1962 and 1974*
First published in this paperback
edition by Methuen and Co Ltd 1967
Second revised edition published by Eyre Methuen 1974
11 New Fetter Lane London EC4P 4EE
Published in Great Britain by
Butler & Tanner Ltd, Frome and London

ISBN 0 413 32670 5

CAUTION

Henrik Johan Ibsen

1828   Born at Skien in south-east Norway on 20 March, the second child of Knud Ibsen, a merchant, and his wife Marichen, *née* Altenburg.

1834–5 Father becomes ruined. The family moves to Venstoep, a few miles outside Skien.

1844   Ibsen (aged fifteen) becomes assistant to an apothecary at Grimstad, a tiny seaport further down the coast. Stays there for six years in great poverty.

1846   Has an illegitimate son with a servant-girl, Else Sofie Jensen.

1849   Writes his first play, CATILINE (in verse).

1850   Leaves Grimstad to become a student in Christiania (now Oslo). Writes second play, THE WARRIOR'S BARROW.

1851   Is invited to join Ole Bull's newly formed National Theatre at Bergen. Does so, and stays six years, writing, directing, designing costumes and keeping the accounts.

1852   Visits Copenhagen and Dresden to learn about the theatre. Writes ST JOHN'S EVE, a romantic comedy in verse and prose.

1853   ST JOHN'S EVE acted at Bergen. Failure.

1854   Writes LADY INGER OF OESTRAAT, an historical tragedy in prose.

1855   LADY INGER OF OESTRAAT acted at Bergen. Failure. Writes THE FEAST AT SOLHAUG, another romantic verse-and-prose comedy.

1856   THE FEAST AT SOLHAUG acted at Bergen. His first
       success. Meets Suzannah Thoresen. Writes OLAF
       LILJEKRANS, a third verse-and-prose comedy.

1857   OLAF LILJEKRANS acted at Bergen. Failure. Leaves
       Bergen to become artistic manager of the Christiania
       Norwegian Theatre. Writes THE VIKINGS AT HEL-
       GELAND, an historical prose tragedy.

1858   Marries Suzannah Thoresen. THE VIKINGS AT HEL-
       GELAND staged. Small success

1859   His only child, Sigurd, born.

1860–1 Years of poverty and despair. Unable to write.

1862   Writes LOVE'S COMEDY, a modern verse satire, his
       first play for five years. It is rejected by his own theatre,
       which goes bankrupt.

1863   Ibsen gets part-time job as literary adviser to the
       Danish-controlled Christiania Theatre. Extremely
       poor. Applies unsuccessfully to Government for
       financial support. Resorts to moneylenders. Writes
       THE PRETENDERS, another historical prose tragedy.
       Is granted a travel stipend by the Government; this
       is augmented by a collection raised by Bjoernson and
       other friends.

1864   THE PRETENDERS staged in Christiania. A success.
       He leaves Norway and settles in Rome. Remains resi-
       dent abroad for the next twenty-seven years. Begins
       EMPEROR AND GALILEAN.

1865   Writes BRAND, in verse (as a play for reading, not
       acting), in Rome and Ariccia.

1866   BRAND published. Immense success; Ibsen becomes
       famous throughout Scandinavia (but it is not acted
       for nineteen years).

1867   Writes PEER GYNT, in verse (also to be read, not

acted), in Rome, Ischia and Sorrento. It, too, is a great success; but is not staged for seven years.

1868   Moves from Rome and settles in Dresden.

1869   Attends opening of Suez Canal as Norwegian delegate Completes THE LEAGUE OF YOUTH, a modern prose comedy.

1871   Revises his shorter poems and issues them in a volume. His farewell to verse; for the rest of his life he publishes exclusively in prose.

1873   Completes (after nine years) EMPEROR AND GALILEAN, his last historical play. Begins to be known in Germany and England.

1874   Returns briefly to Norway for first time in ten years. The students hold a torchlight procession in his honour.

1875   Leaves Dresden after seven years and settles in Munich. Begins THE PILLARS OF SOCIETY, the first of his twelve great modern prose dramas.

1876   PEER GYNT staged for first time. THE VIKINGS AT HELGELAND is performed in Munich, the first of his plays to be staged outside Scandinavia.

1877   Completes THE PILLARS OF SOCIETY. This makes him famous in Germany, where it is widely acted.

1878   Returns to Italy for a year.

1879   Writes A DOLL'S HOUSE in Rome and Amalfi. It causes an immediate sensation, though a decade elapses before it makes Ibsen internationally famous. Returns for a year to Munich.

1880   Resettles in Italy for a further five years. First performance of an Ibsen play in England (THE PILLARS OF SOCIETY for a single matinee in London).

1881   Writes GHOSTS in Rome and Sorrento. Violently attacked; all theatres reject it, and bookshops return it to the publisher.

1882   Writes AN ENEMY OF THE PEOPLE in Rome. Cordially received. GHOSTS receives its first performance (in Chicago).

1884   Writes THE WILD DUCK in Rome and Gossensass. It, and all his subsequent plays, were regarded as obscure and were greeted with varying degrees of bewilderment.

1885   Revisits Norway again, for the first time since 1874. Leaves Rome and resettles in Munich.

1886   Writes ROSMERSHOLM in Munich.

1888   Writes THE LADY FROM THE SEA in Munich.

1889   Meets and becomes infatuated with the eighteen-year-old Emilie Bardach in Gossensass. Does not see her again, but the experience shadows the remainder of his writing. Janet Achurch acts Nora in London, the first major English-speaking production of Ibsen.

1890   Writes HEDDA GABLER in Munich.

1891   Returns to settle permanently in Norway.

1892   Writes THE MASTER BUILDER in Christiania.

1894   Writes LITTLE EYOLF in Christiania.

1896   Writes JOHN GABRIEL BORKMAN in Christiania.

1899   Writes WHEN WE DEAD AWAKEN in Christiania.

1901   First stroke. Partly paralysed.

1903   Second stroke. Left largely helpless.

1906   Dies in Christiania on 23 May, aged seventy-eight.

Introduction

Hedda Gabler occupies a curious, almost anachronistic position in the Ibsen cycle. He wrote it in 1890, between *The Lady from the Sea* and *The Master Builder*, but if one had to date it from internal evidence one would be tempted to place it ten years earlier, as a companion piece to *A Doll's House*, *Ghosts* and *An Enemy of the People*. Like them, it is written very simply and directly; we feel, as in those plays, that he is working within an illuminated circle and not, as in the plays of his final period from *The Lady from the Sea* onwards, that he is exploring the darkness outside that circle. At first sight, again, it appears to differ from these final plays in not being an exercise in self-analysis. This, however, is an illusion, for if we examine *Hedda Gabler* closely we find that it contains one of the most revealing self-portraits he ever painted. The play might, indeed, be subtitled 'Portrait of the Dramatist as a Young Woman'.

The circumstances under which he wrote *Hedda Gabler* were as follows. In the summer of 1889, while holidaying at Gossensass in the Tyrol, Ibsen, then aged sixty-one, had become violently infatuated with an eighteen-year-old Viennese girl named Emilie Bardach. After his return to Munich in September, they wrote to each other continuously for four months; then Ibsen broke off the correspondence, and apart from two brief letters towards the end of the year and a third, seven years later, in acknowledgement of a telegram of congratulations, he did not contact her again. Two years later he was to use this relationship of mutual infatuation as the basis for *The Master Builder*, but the change it wrought on Ibsen was immediate. For years he had deliberately suppressed his own emotional life, an undersized and ugly man resigned to a loveless marriage; but his encounter with Emilie had awoken him to the realization

that, as Mr Graham Greene has recently remarked, fame
is a powerful aphrodisiac, and he now entered on a series of
romantic relationships with women thirty to forty years his
junior. (Indeed, the second of these, with the artist Helene
Raff, began while he was still corresponding with Emilie.)

It is unlikely, however, that any of these relationships ever
resulted in a physical affair, and this meant that, while im-
mensely enriching his work, they also introduced into it a
strong undertone of pessimism. In 1887, in a speech in Stockholm, he had startled his audience by describing himself as an
'optimist', and *The Lady from the Sea*, written in 1888, had
reflected this optimism. 'After so many tragedies,' Edmund
Gosse had written on its appearance, 'this is a comedy . . . the
tone is quite unusually sunny, and without a tinge of pessimism. It is in some respects the reverse of *Rosmersholm*, the
bitterness of restrained and balked individuality, which ends
in death, being contrasted with the sweetness of emancipated
and gratified individuality, which leads to health and peace.'
But none of his five subsequent plays could by any possible
stretch of the imagination be described as comedies. The mood
of *Hedda Gabler*, *The Master Builder*, *Little Eyolf*, *John Gabriel
Borkman* and *When We Dead Awaken* is, like that of *Rosmersholm*, 'restrained and balked individuality', and I do not
think there can be much doubt that this stems from the
realization that for various reasons (fear of scandal, sense of
duty towards his wife, consciousness of old age, perhaps the
consciousness or fear of physical impotence), he, who had
suppressed his emotional life for so long, now had the oppor-
tunities to fulfil it, but was unable to take advantage of them.
As a result of his meeting with Emilie Bardach a new glory,
but also a new darkness, entered into his work.

He began to plan a new play immediately on his return from
Gossensass. Only a week after arriving in Munich, on 7 October
1889, he wrote to Emilie: 'A new poem begins to dawn in me.
I want to work on it this winter, transmuting into it the glowing

inspiration of the summer. But the end may be disappointment. I feel it. It is my way.' A week later, on 15 October, he wrote to her: 'My imagination is ragingly at work, but always straying to where in working hours it should not. I cannot keep down the memories of the summer, neither do I want to. The things we have lived through I live again and again – and still again. To make of them a poem is for the time being impossible. For the time being? Shall I ever succeed in the future? And do I really wish that I could and would so succeed? For the moment, at any rate, I cannot.' However, on 19 November he wrote more cheerfully: 'I am greatly preoccupied with the preparations for my new play. Sit tight at my desk the whole day. Go out only towards evening. I dream and remember and write.'

Unfortunately, we do not know whether the play he was working on at this time was in fact *Hedda Gabler*. Ibsen left eight sets of rough notes dating from around this period; most of them obviously refer to *Hedda Gabler*, but some seem to point towards *The Master Builder* and others towards a third play which he never ultimately wrote, and since these notes are undated we cannot be sure to which of the three projects he was referring in his letters to Emilie. Some scholars think he did not begin to plan *Hedda* until April 1890; others believe he had already conceived it as early as February 1889. At any rate, by the spring of 1890 Ibsen's plans for *Hedda* were sufficiently advanced for him to express the hope that he would have his first draft ready by midsummer, so that he would be able to work on it during his summer holiday in (again) Gossensass. But on 29 June 1890 he wrote to Carl Snoilsky, the Swedish poet (generally assumed to be the original of Rosmer) that the play had not worked out and that he was staying in Munich until he could get the first draft finished. Perhaps he feared Gossensass might awake disturbing memories.

As things turned out, he did not complete the first draft of even Act 1 until 10 August. On 13 August he began Act 2, but early in September he scrapped this, and on 6 September he began a new draft of this act. Things now went better, for by 7 October he had completed the draft not only of Act 2 but also of Acts 3 and 4. The play was at this stage entitled simply *Hedda*, and the draft in which it exists bears all the appearance of having been made as a fair copy to send to the printer. But he was not satisfied, and rewrote the play thoroughly, introducing into it for the first time many of its most striking and famous features. This revisionary work occupied him until 18 November, and *Hedda Gabler*, as he now entitled it, to underline the fact that she was her father's daughter rather than her husband's wife, was published by Gyldendal of Copenhagen on 16 December 1890, only just in time for the Christmas sales – always an important consideration with Ibsen, who depended on book sales in Scandinavia for a large proportion of his income.[1]

As with every play he wrote after *A Doll's House* in 1879, excepting only the comparatively light and simple *Enemy of the People*, the public reaction was one of utter bewilderment. Halvdan Koht, in his introduction (1934) to the play in the centenary edition of Ibsen's works, has described how Norway received it. 'Its only message seemed to be despair. No meaning nor purpose, simply a suicide ending an absolutely pointless life. . . . In contemporary criticisms the most common word used to describe the main character is "puzzling", "improbable" or "incredible". Readers got the impression that in the concluding line of the play – "But, good God! People don't do such things!" – Ibsen was making fun of them; for it reminded them that too many of them had said just that about Nora's final action in *A Doll's House*. There were things in *Hedda Gabler* that seemed almost intended to parody *A Doll's*

[1] His plays, though widely staged, were usually put on for a few performances only. For example, it was not until 1925 that any English production of Ibsen achieved a run of fifty performances.

House – for example, Hedda's lie about having destroyed the manuscript to help her husband, or the curious form of "comradeship" between man and woman portrayed here.' Bredo Morgenstierna wrote in *Aftenposten* of 'the obscurity, the eccentric and abnormal psychology, the empty and desolate impression which the whole picture leaves', while Alfred Sinding-Larsen in *Morgenbladet* described Hedda herself as 'a horrid miscarriage of the imagination, a monster in female form to whom no parallel can be found in real life'.

Nor, as with some of his plays (e.g. *Ghosts*), were people much enlightened when *Hedda Gabler* was performed. At the première on 31 January 1891, at the Residenztheater, Munich, the public whistled. Ibsen was present and was much displeased at the declamatory manner of the actress who played Hedda. On 10 February there was a rather better performance at the Lessing Theatre in Berlin, but even here neither the public nor the critics seem to have understood the play. Nor was it a success in Stockholm or Gothenburg, while in Copenhagen on 25 February it was a complete fiasco, being greeted by hissing, whistling and laughter. The following evening it was given in Christiania, also inadequately. The first respectable performance of *Hedda Gabler* was, improbably, in London (20 April 1891), where, although it called forth the usual stream of abuse from the popular newspapers ('What a horrible story! What a hideous play!' wrote Clement Scott in the *Daily Telegraph*, and the *Pictorial World* commented: 'The play is simply a bad escape of moral sewage-gas . . . Hedda's soul is a-crawl with the foulest passions of humanity'), intelligent opinion was considerably impressed. Henry James, who had been puzzled by *Hedda Gabler* on reading it, found the performance gratifyingly illuminating. 'The play on perusal', he wrote (*On the Occasion of Hedda Gabler*, 1891), 'left one comparatively muddled and mystified, fascinated but – in one's intellectual sympathy – snubbed. Acted, it leads that sympathy over the straightest of roads with all the exhilaration of a superior pace.'

But he added a gentle rider. 'Much more, I confess, one doesn't get from it; but an hour of refreshing exercise is a reward in itself. . . . Ibsen is various, and *Hedda Gabler* is probably an ironical pleasantry, the artistic exercise of a mind saturated with the vision of human infirmities; saturated, above all, with a sense of the infinitude, for all its mortal savour, of *character*, finding that an endless romance and a perpetual challenge. Can there have been at the source of such a production a mere refinement of conscious power, an enjoyment of difficulty and a preconceived victory over it?'

There are many people who share James's view of *Hedda Gabler* as a brilliant but, for Ibsen, curiously detached, objective, almost brutal 'exercise' – a view which has been greatly fostered by the tendency of actresses to portray Hedda as an evil genius, a kind of suburban Lady Macbeth. The opposite view, that it is one of Ibsen's most 'committed' plays, has been brilliantly argued by Dr Arne Duve in his wayward but stimulating book *Symbolikken i Henrik Ibsens Skuespill* (Nasjonalforlaget, Oslo, 1945). Dr Duve suggests that Hedda represents Ibsen's repressed and crippled emotional life. As a young man, he reminds us, Ibsen had been wildly emotional; at eighteen he had fathered an illegitimate child, and at least once during those early years he became a near-alcoholic and is believed to have attempted suicide. Loevborg and Tesman, Dr Duve argues, are aspects of Ibsen's own self; Loevborg is an idealized portrait of himself as he had been in the wild years of his youth, Tesman a *reductio ad absurdum* of what he had chosen to become. Loevborg stands for Ibsen's emotional self, Tesman for his intellectual self. Ibsen was haunted throughout the latter half of his life by the feeling that he had stifled his emotional self and that only his bourgeois and slightly ludicrous intellectual self had lived on. He had persuaded himself to accept this state of affairs, but the encounter with Emilie Bardach seems to have brought all his old feelings of guilt rushing to the surface. Hedda longs to be like Loevborg, but lacks the courage; she is repelled by the reality of sex (as Ibsen himself was?) and prefers to experience it vicariously by encouraging Loevborg to describe his experiences to her. Two emotions are dominant in her, the fear of scandal and the fear of ridicule, and Ibsen himself, though always willing to trail his coat in print, seems also to have been privately dominated by these emotions.

But if *Hedda Gabler* is, in fact, a self-portrait, it is certainly an unconscious one – not that that makes it any the less truthful or valuable; rather the reverse. Ibsen's rough preliminary jottings referred to above make it clear that he *intended* the play as a tragedy of the purposelessness of life, and in particular of the purposelessness imposed on women of his time both by their upbringing and by the social conventions which limited their activities. The following extracts will serve as examples:

'(1) They aren't all created to be mothers.

(2) They all have a leaning towards sensuality, but are afraid of the scandal.

(3) They realize that life holds a purpose for them, but they cannot find that purpose.'

'Women have no influence on public affairs. So they want to influence individuals spiritually.'

'The great tragedy of life is that so many people have nothing to do but yearn for happiness without ever being able to find it.'

'Men and women don't belong to the same century.'

'There are very few true parents in the world. Most people are brought up by uncles or aunts – neglected or misunderstood or spoiled.'

'The play is to be about "the insuperable"—the longing and striving to defy convention, to defy what people accept (including Hedda).'

'Hedda is typical of women in her position and with her

character. One marries Tesman but one titillates one's imagination with Eilert Loevborg. One leans back in one's chair, closes one's eyes and pictures to oneself his adventures. The enormous difference: Mrs Elvsted "works to improve him morally", while for Hedda he is merely a subject for cowardly and tantalizing dreams. She lacks the courage to partake actively in such going-on. Then her confession as to how she really feels. Tied! Don't understand – But to be an object of ridicule! Of ridicule!'

'The daemon in Hedda is that she wants to influence another human being, but once that has happened, she despises him.'

'Loevborg has leanings towards Bohemianism. Hedda is also attracted to it, but dares not take the jump.'

'It's really a man's life she wants to lead. In all respects. But then scruples intervene. Some inherited – some implanted.'

'Remember I was born the child of an old man. And not merely old. Played-out – or anyway, decrepit. Perhaps that has left its mark.'

'It is a great delusion that one only loves one person.'

'Tesman represents propriety. Hedda represents *ennui*. Mrs R. [i.e. Mrs Elvsted] modern nervousness and hysteria. Brack the representative of bourgeois society.'

'H.L. [i.e. Loevborg]'s despair arises from the fact that he wants to control the world but cannot control himself.'

'Life for Hedda is a farce which isn't worth seeing through to the end.'

As usual with Ibsen's plays, certain elements in *Hedda Gabler* can be traced to incidents in the lives of people whom he knew personally or had heard or read about. For example, when he visited Norway in 1885 he must have heard of the marriage the previous winter between a famous beauty named Sophie Magelssen and the philologist Peter Groth. Groth had married her on a research grant which he had won in competition with Hjalmar Falk, whom many thought the better scholar of the two (and who gets a consolatory mention in the play as the dead Cabinet Minister who had previously owned the Tesmans' villa). Neither Tesman nor Loevborg, however, was modelled on either of these two. Ibsen told his son Sigurd that he had based Tesman on Julius Elias, a young German student of literature whom he had got to know in Munich. Elias's great passion was for 'putting other people's papers in order'; later he became a distinguished man of letters, and ironically enough it fell to him to put Ibsen's own papers in order when he shared with Halvdan Koht the task of editing the dramatist's literary remains.[1] Loevborg was closely modelled on a Dane named Julius Hoffory who was Professor of Scandinavian Philology and Phonetics in Berlin. Hoffory was a gifted but unbalanced man who mixed freely with women of low repute and had once lost the manuscript of a book during a nocturnal orgy. He recognized himself delightedly when *Hedda Gabler* appeared, and thereafter adopted Loevborg as his pseudonym.

Miss Tesman, George's aunt, was based on an old lady from Trondhejm named Elise Hokk. Ibsen had met her a number of times during the early seventies in Dresden, where she tended a sick sister for three years until the latter died. He wrote a charming poem in tribute to her in 1874. She is the only character in the play, as far as is known, who was based on a Norwegian original, and this may have influenced early critics who wrote that *Hedda Gabler* was the least Norwegian of Ibsen's plays and that the town (unnamed as usual) in which the action takes place was less suggestive of Christiania than of a Continental capital. William Archer, however, who knew Christiania well, felt sure that Ibsen had that city in mind, and

---

[1] In fairness to Elias, it should be stated that Tesman is a much less ridiculous character in the early draft of the play than Ibsen subsequently made him. His maddening repetition of nursery phrases such as 'Fancy that!' was added during revision.

added the interesting comment that Ibsen, although writing in 1890, seemed to have set the play some thirty years earlier. 'The electric cars, telephones and other conspicuous factors in the life of a modern capital', he wrote in his introduction (1907) to the English translation by himself and Edmund Gosse, 'are notably absent from the play. There is no electric light in Secretary Falk's villa. It is still the habit for ladies to return on foot from evening parties, with gallant swains escorting them. This "suburbanism" which so distressed the London critics of 1891, was characteristic of the Christiania Ibsen himself had known in the eighteen-sixties – the Christiania of *Love's Comedy* – rather than of the greatly extended and modernised city of the end of the century.'

Three further incidents which came to Ibsen's notice found their way into the play. While he was actually working on it, a young married couple came to seek his advice; their happiness, they said, had been ruined because the husband had been hypnotized by another woman. Then there was the unfortunate case of the Norwegian composer Johan Svendsen, whose wife, Sally, in a fit of rage at discovering a letter from another woman hidden in a bouquet of flowers, had burned the score of a symphony which he had just composed. Finally, he heard of the even more unfortunate incident of the Norwegian lady whose husband had cured himself of drink and had resolved never to touch it again. To see how much power she had over him, she rolled a keg of brandy into his room as a birthday present, and before the day was over he was dead drunk. All these episodes are reflected in *Hedda Gabler*.

The original of Hedda herself is not known. She has been rather glibly assumed by some critics to be a portrait of Emilie, on the grounds that both were beautiful and aristocratic and did not know what to do with their lives, and that Ibsen's description of Hedda (aristocratic face, fine complexion, veiled expression in the eyes, etc.) corresponds to early photographs of Emilie. The same characteristics could, however, be found in the photograph of almost any well-born young lady of the period; the description would apply equally to Queen Alexandra; and few women of Ibsen's time, let alone girls of eighteen knew what to do with their lives. In any case, the idea of creating such a character had been at the back of Ibsen's mind long before he met Emilie, for his rough notes for *Rosmersholm* (1886) contain a sketch of a girl, intended as Rosmer's elder daughter, though he finally decided not to include her in the play, who 'is in danger of succumbing to inactivity and loneliness. She has rich talents which are lying unused.' On the other hand, Emilie must certainly have been at the back of his mind when he was writing *Hedda Gabler*, and it is possible that Hedda may be a portrait, conscious or unconscious, of what Emilie might become in ten years if she did not marry the right man or find a fixed purpose in life. If so, it was a prophecy that came uncomfortably near the truth, for Emilie, though she lived to be eighty-three – she died as late as 1 November 1955 – accomplished nothing and never married.

The differences between Ibsen's first draft and his final version as we know it are, as has already been remarked, numerous and revealing. Apart from changing Tesman from an ordinary bourgeois husband into a ninny spoiled (like Hjalmar Ekdal) by loving aunts, he improved him morally, for in the first draft it is Tesman who suggests hiding the manuscript to give Loevborg a fright, and so is partly responsible for the latter's death. Miss Tesman's important account to Bertha in Act 1 of Hedda's life with her father was an afterthought; so were Mademoiselle Danielle, Mrs Elvsted's abundant hair and Hedda's jealousy of it, the image of the vine-leaves, and Hedda's threat (before the play opens) to shoot Loevborg. Act 1 ends much less strongly in the draft, with no mention of the pistols; and Tesman and Mrs Elvsted both know of Hedda's former close relationship with Loevborg. Miss Tesman's role is less complex than in the final version; she does

not realize in Act 1 that Hedda is going to have a baby, and
has a far less effective scene with Hedda in Act 4. The conversation between Hedda, Loevborg and Tesman over the photograph album about the honeymoon contains a direct reference
of Gossensass, subsequently deleted. And Brack, in a passage
which one is rather sorry to lose, describes sadly to Hedda
how three 'triangles' of which he was a part have been broken
up during the past six months – not, as Hedda guesses, by
other bachelors but by intruders far more destructive to extra-
marital relationships – children. Finally, one may note two
remarks which Ibsen originally put into Hedda's mouth but
subsequently deleted: (1) 'I can't understand how anyone
could fall in love with a man who isn't married – or engaged –
or at least in love with someone else.' (2) 'To take someone
from someone else – I think that must be so wonderful!' He
saved these thoughts for a character, already created in minia-
ture in *The Lady from the Sea*, to whom he was to allot the
principal female role in his next play two years later – Hilde
Wangel in *The Master Builder*.

The repeated references to the 'vine-leaves' continue to
puzzle critics, even though William Archer cleared the problem up fifty years ago. 'Surely', he wrote, 'this is a very
obvious image or symbol of the beautiful, the ideal, aspect of
bacchic elation and revelry. . . . Professor Dietrichson relates
that among the young artists whose society Ibsen frequented
during his first years in Rome it was customary, at their little
festivals, for the revellers to deck themselves in this fashion.
But the image is so obvious that there is no need to trace it to
any personal experience. The attempt to place Hedda's vine-
leaves among Ibsen's obscurities is an example of the firm
resolution not to understand which animated the criticism of
the nineties.' Not, alas, only of the nineties. The picture
which the vine-leaves are intended to evoke is that of the
young god, 'burning and unashamed', in Hedda's words;
as Archer noted, it was an image which Ibsen had used

previously in both *Peer Gynt* and *Emperor and Galilean.*

A point that is sometimes missed in production of *Hedda Gabler* is the importance of correct casting for Bertha, the Tesmans' maid. Ibsen never created a role, however tiny, that was not both integral to the play and rewarding to the player, and his servants are no exceptions – one thinks of the two butlers, the superior Pettersen and the inferior Jensen, in *The Wild Duck*, the housekeeper Mrs Helseth in *Rosmersholm*, and Malene, the sour maid in *John Gabriel Borkman*. Ibsen underlined Bertha's importance in a letter which he wrote to Kristine Steen on 14 January 1891 concerning the casting of the play for Christiania. 'Mrs Wolf', he wrote, 'wishes to be released from playing the maid Bertha in my new play, since she is of the opinion that this role could be adequately filled by any other member of the company. She is mistaken. There is no-one else at the theatre who can perform Bertha as I wish her to be performed. Only Mrs Wolf can do it. She has evidently not taken the trouble to read the play carefully, or she could hardly fail to appreciate this. George Tesman, his old aunts and Bertha together create a picture of completeness and unity. They have common thoughts, common memories, a common attitude towards life. To Hedda they represent a force foreign and hostile to her and to everything she stands for. The harmony that exists between them must be apparent on the stage. And this can be achieved if Mrs Wolf plays the part. But only if she does. My respect for Mrs Wolf's soundness of judgment is too great for me seriously to believe that she regards it as artistically beneath her to create a servant. I did not regard it as artistically beneath me to create this honest, artless old creature. Here in Munich this unpretentious character is to be created by one of the Hoftheater's leading actresses, and she has embraced the task with love and interest. Besides being an actress, she is also an artist. By this I mean that she regards it as a matter of honour not merely to "give a performance" but to turn a created character into a thing of flesh and blood.' Ibsen's plea fell, however, on deaf ears, for Mrs Wolf still refused to play the part.

Despite its early failures on the stages of Europe, *Hedda Gabler* has come to be accepted as one of the most popular of Ibsen's plays. London has seen no less than nineteen separate productions, a number exceeded only, among Ibsen's other plays, by *A Doll's House* and *Ghosts*. Among the actresses who have played it there are Elizabeth Robins (1891 and 1893), Eleonora Duse (in Italian, 1903), Mrs Patrick Campbell (1907 and 1922), Lydia Yavorska (in Russian, 1909, and in English, 1911), Jean Forbes-Robertson (1931, 1936 and 1951), Sonia Dresdel (1942 and 1943), Peggy Ashcroft (1954) and Maggie Smith (1970). Probably the finest English Hedda, however, was Pamela Brown, who in 1941, at the age of twenty-two, gave a performance at the Oxford Playhouse which caused James Agate seriously to compare her with the young Sarah Bernhardt. 'The moment that unquiet spirit appeared in the curtain'd doorway, drew a long breath, and paused to survey the Tesmanesque scene in marble, cold disfavour', he wrote, 'why, then we knew that Hedda was going to be present. . . . I was not playgoing in 1867, when She Who Must Not Be Named was 22, which is the age of Miss Pamela Brown. But as that great player must have been in her experimental years, so is this young actress now'. Another admired and acclaimed performance in the role was that of Catherine Lacey at the Bristol Old Vic in 1948. America first saw the play on 30 March 1898, when Elizabeth Robins presented a single performance at the Fifth Avenue Theatre in New York. *The Critic* wrote of this production that 'it was, on the whole, the most satisfactory representation of an Ibsen play ever given in this city', and described Miss Robins's performance as 'in every way a remarkable achievement'. Unfortunately, according to Norman Hapgood in *The Stage in America, 1897–1900*, 'it failed to interest the public enough to continue contemplated Ibsen experiments'. Blanche Bates played it for a single matinée in Washington in 1900; then in 1903 Minnie Fiske presented it in New York for a whole week to crowded houses, and brought it back to the Manhattan Theatre in November 1904, when it achieved the, by the standard of those days, considerable number of twenty-six performances. The cast included George Arliss as Judge Brack. In 1905 Alla Nazimova played it at the Russian Theatre, New York, in Russian, and the following year she performed it in English, creating a tremendous impression. Subsequent Heddas in New York have included Emily Stevens, Eva le Gallienne, Tallulah Bankhead (on television), Anne Meacham and Claire Bloom.

MICHAEL MEYER

This translation of *Hedda Gabler* was first performed on 9 November 1960 at the 4th Street Theatre, New York, in a production by David Ross with Anne Meacham as Hedda. The first London performance was on 29 June 1970 at the Cambridge Theatre, under the auspices of the National Theatre. The cast was:

GEORGE TESMAN, research graduate in cultural history	Jeremy Brett
HEDDA TESMAN, his wife	Maggie Smith
MISS JULIANA TESMAN, his aunt	Jeanne Watts
MRS ELVSTED	Sheila Reid
JUDGE BRACK	John Moffat
EILERT LOEVBORG	Robert Stephens
BERTHA, a maid	Julia McCarthy

Designed by Mago

Directed by Ingmar Bergman

The action takes place in TESMAN's villa in the fashionable quarter of town.

Act One

*A large drawing-room, handsomely and tastefully furnished;
decorated in dark colours. In the rear wall is a broad open doorway, with curtains drawn back to either side. It leads to a smaller
room, decorated in the same style as the drawing-room. In the
right-hand wall of the drawing-room a folding door leads out to
the hall. The opposite wall, on the left, contains french windows,
also with curtains drawn back on either side. Through the glass
we can see part of a veranda, and trees in autumn colours.
Downstage stands an oval table, covered by a cloth and surrounded
by chairs. Downstage right, against the wall, is a broad stove tiled
with dark porcelain; in front of it stand a high-backed armchair,
a cushioned footrest and two footstools. Upstage right, in an
alcove, is a corner sofa, with a small, round table. Downstage left,
a little away from the wall, is another sofa. Upstage of the french
windows, a piano. On either side of the open doorway in the rear
wall stand what-nots holding ornaments of terra-cotta and
majolica. Against the rear wall of the smaller room can be seen a
sofa, a table and a couple of chairs. Above this sofa hangs the
portrait of a handsome old man in general's uniform. Above the
table a lamp hangs from the ceiling, with a shade of opalescent,
milky glass. All round the drawing-room bunches of flowers stand
in vases and glasses. More bunches lie on the tables. The floors of
both rooms are covered with thick carpets. Morning light. The
sun shines in through the french windows.*

MISS JULIANA TESMAN, *wearing a hat and carrying a parasol, enters from the hall, followed by* BERTHA, *who is carrying
a bunch of flowers wrapped in paper.* MISS TESMAN *is about
sixty-five, of pleasant and kindly appearance. She is neatly
but simply dressed in grey outdoor clothes.* BERTHA, *the maid,
is rather simple and rustic-looking. She is getting on in years.*

MISS TESMAN (*stops just inside the door, listens, and says in a hushed voice*). Well, fancy that! They're not up yet!

BERTHA (*also in hushed tones*). What did I tell you, miss? The boat didn't get in till midnight. And when they did turn up – Jesus, miss, you should have seen all the things madam made me unpack before she'd go to bed!

MISS TESMAN. Ah, well. Let them have a good lie in. But let's have some nice fresh air waiting for them when they do come down. (*Goes to the french windows and throws them wide open.*)

BERTHA (*bewildered at the table, the bunch of flowers in her hand*). I'm blessed if there's a square inch left to put anything. I'll have to let it lie here, miss. (*Puts it on the piano.*)

MISS TESMAN. Well, Bertha dear, so now you have a new mistress. Heaven knows it nearly broke my heart to have to part with you.

BERTHA (*snivels*). What about me, Miss Juju? How do you suppose I felt? After all the happy years I've spent with you and Miss Rena?

MISS TESMAN. We must accept it bravely, Bertha. It was the only way. George needs you to take care of him. He could never manage without you. You've looked after him ever since he was a tiny boy.

BERTHA. Oh, but, Miss Juju, I can't help thinking about Miss Rena, lying there all helpless, poor dear. And that new girl! She'll never learn the proper way to handle an invalid.

MISS TESMAN. Oh, I'll manage to train her. I'll do most of the work myself, you know. You needn't worry about my poor sister, Bertha dear.

BERTHA. But, Miss Juju, there's another thing. I'm frightened madam may not find me suitable.

MISS TESMAN. Oh, nonsense, Bertha. There may be one or two little things to begin with –

BERTHA. She's a real lady. Wants everything just so.

MISS TESMAN. But of course she does! General Gabler's daughter! Think of what she was accustomed to when the general was alive. You remember how we used to see her out riding with her father? In that long black skirt? With the feather in her hat?

BERTHA. Oh, yes, miss. As if I could forget! But, Lord! I never dreamed I'd live to see a match between her and Master Georgie.

MISS TESMAN. Neither did I. By the way, Bertha, from now on you must stop calling him Master Georgie. You must say Dr Tesman.

BERTHA. Yes, madam said something about that too. Last night – the moment they'd set foot inside the door. Is it true, then, miss?

MISS TESMAN. Indeed it is. Just fancy, Bertha, some foreigners have made him a doctor. It happened while they were away. I had no idea till he told me when they got off the boat.

BERTHA. Well, I suppose there's no limit to what he won't become. He's that clever. I never thought he'd go in for hospital work, though.

MISS TESMAN. No, he's not that kind of doctor. (*Nods impressively.*) In any case, you may soon have to address him by an even grander title.

BERTHA. You don't say! What might that be, miss?

MISS TESMAN (*smiles*). Ah! If you only knew! (*Moved.*) Dear God, if only poor Joachim could rise out of his grave and see what his little son has grown into! (*Looks round.*) But, Bertha, why have you done this? Taken the chintz covers off all the furniture!

BERTHA. Madam said I was to. Can't stand chintz covers on chairs, she said.

MISS TESMAN. But surely they're not going to use this room as a parlour?

BERTHA. So I gathered, miss. From what madam said. He didn't say anything. The Doctor.

GEORGE TESMAN *comes into the rear room from the right, humming, with an open, empty travelling-bag in his hand. He is about thirty-three, of medium height and youthful appearance, rather plump, with an open, round, contented face, and fair hair and beard. He wears spectacles, and is dressed in comfortable indoor clothes.*

MISS TESMAN. Good morning! Good morning, George!

TESMAN (*in open doorway*). Auntie Juju! Dear Auntie Juju! (*Comes forward and shakes her hand.*) You've come all the way out here! And so early! What?

MISS TESMAN. Well, I had to make sure you'd settled in comfortably.

TESMAN. But you can't have had a proper night's sleep.

MISS TESMAN. Oh, never mind that.

TESMAN. We were so sorry we couldn't give you a lift. But you saw how it was – Hedda had so much luggage – and she insisted on having it all with her.

MISS TESMAN. Yes, I've never seen so much luggage.

BERTHA (*to* TESMAN). Shall I go and ask madam if there's anything I can lend her a hand with?

TESMAN. Er – thank you, Bertha, no, you needn't bother. She says if she wants you for anything she'll ring.

BERTHA (*over to right*). Oh. Very good.

TESMAN. Oh, Bertha – take this bag, will you?

BERTHA (*takes it*). I'll put it in the attic.

She goes out into the hall.

TESMAN. Just fancy, Auntie Juju, I filled that whole bag with notes for my book. You know, it's really incredible what I've managed to find rooting through those archives. By Jove! Wonderful old things no one even knew existed –

MISS TESMAN. I'm sure you didn't waste a single moment of your honeymoon, George dear.

TESMAN. No, I think I can truthfully claim that. But, Auntie

Juju, do take your hat off. Here. Let me untie it for you.
What?

MISS TESMAN (*as he does so*). Oh dear, oh dear! It's just as if
you were still living at home with us.

TESMAN (*turns the hat in his hand and looks at it*). I say! What
a splendid new hat!

MISS TESMAN. I bought it for Hedda's sake.

TESMAN. For Hedda's sake? What?

MISS TESMAN. So that Hedda needn't be ashamed of me, in
case we ever go for a walk together.

TESMAN (*pats her cheek*). You still think of everything, don't
you, Auntie Juju? (*Puts the hat down on a chair by the table.*)
Come on, let's sit down here on the sofa. And have a little
chat while we wait for Hedda.

They sit. She puts her parasol in the corner of the sofa.

MISS TESMAN (*clasps both his hands and looks at him*). Oh,
George, it's so wonderful to have you back, and be able to
see you with my own eyes again! Poor dear Joachim's own
son!

TESMAN. What about me? It's wonderful for me to see you
again, Auntie Juju. You've been a mother to me. And a
father, too.

MISS TESMAN. You'll always keep a soft spot in your heart for
your old aunties, won't you, George dear?

TESMAN. I suppose Auntie Rena's no better? What?

MISS TESMAN. Alas, no. I'm afraid she'll never get better, poor
dear. She's lying there just as she has for all these years.
Please God I may be allowed to keep her for a little longer.
If I lost her I don't know what I'd do. Especially now I
haven't you to look after.

TESMAN (*pats her on the back*). There, there, there!

MISS TESMAN (*with a sudden change of mood*). Oh, but, George,
fancy you being a married man! And to think it's you who've

won Hedda Gabler! The beautiful Hedda Gabler! Fancy! She was always so surrounded by admirers.

TESMAN (*hums a little and smiles contentedly*). Yes, I suppose there are quite a few people in this town who wouldn't mind being in my shoes. What?

MISS TESMAN. And what a honeymoon! Five months! Nearly six.

TESMAN. Well, I've done a lot of work, you know. All those archives to go through. And I've had to read lots of books.

MISS TESMAN. Yes, dear, of course. (*Lowers her voice confidentially.*) But tell me, George – haven't you any – any extra little piece of news to give me?

TESMAN. You mean, arising out of the honeymoon?

MISS TESMAN. Yes.

TESMAN. No, I don't think there's anything I didn't tell you in my letters. My doctorate, of course – but I told you about that last night, didn't I?

MISS TESMAN. Yes, yes, I didn't mean that kind of thing. I was just wondering – are you – are you expecting–?

TESMAN. Expecting what?

MISS TESMAN. Oh, come on, George, I'm your old aunt!

TESMAN. Well, actually – yes, I am expecting something.

MISS TESMAN. I knew it!

TESMAN. You'll be happy to learn that before very long I expect to become a – professor.

MISS TESMAN. Professor?

TESMAN. I think I may say that the matter has been decided. But, Auntie Juju, you know about this.

MISS TESMAN (*gives a little laugh*). Yes, of course. I'd forgotten. (*Changes her tone.*) But we were talking about your honeymoon. It must have cost a dreadful amount of money, George?

TESMAN. Oh well, you know, that big research grant I got helped a good deal.

MISS TESMAN. But how on earth did you manage to make it do for two?

TESMAN. Well, to tell the truth it was a bit tricky. What?

MISS TESMAN. Especially when one's travelling with a lady. A little bird tells me that makes things very much more expensive.

TESMAN. Well, yes, of course it does make things a little more expensive. But Hedda has to do things in style, Auntie Juju. I mean, she has to. Anything less grand wouldn't have suited her.

MISS TESMAN. No, no, I suppose not. A honeymoon abroad seems to be the vogue nowadays. But tell me, have you had time to look round the house?

TESMAN. You bet. I've been up since the crack of dawn.

MISS TESMAN. Well, what do you think of it?

TESMAN. Splendid. Absolutely splendid. I'm only wondering what we're going to do with those two empty rooms between that little one and Hedda's bedroom.

MISS TESMAN (*laughs slyly*). Ah, George dear, I'm sure you'll manage to find some use for them – in time.

TESMAN. Yes, of course, Auntie Juju, how stupid of me. You're thinking of my books? What?

MISS TESMAN. Yes, yes, dear boy. I was thinking of your books.

TESMAN. You know, I'm so happy for Hedda's sake that we've managed to get this house. Before we became engaged she often used to say this was the only house in town she felt she could really bear to live in. It used to belong to Mrs Falk – you know, the Prime Minister's widow.

MISS TESMAN. Fancy that! And what a stroke of luck it happened to come into the market. Just as you'd left on your honeymoon.

TESMAN. Yes, Auntie Juju, we've certainly had all the luck with us. What?

MISS TESMAN. But, George dear, the expense! It's going to make a dreadful hole in your pocket, all this.

TESMAN (*a little downcast*). Yes, I – I suppose it will, won't it?

MISS TESMAN. Oh, George, really!

TESMAN. How much do you think it'll cost? Roughly, I mean? What?

MISS TESMAN. I can't possibly say till I see the bills.

TESMAN. Well, luckily Judge Brack's managed to get it on very favourable terms. He wrote and told Hedda so.

MISS TESMAN. Don't you worry, George dear. Anyway, I've stood security for all the furniture and carpets.

TESMAN. Security? But dear, sweet Auntie Juju, how could you possibly stand security?

MISS TESMAN. I've arranged a mortgage on our annuity.

TESMAN (*jumps up*). What? On your annuity? And – Auntie Rena's?

MISS TESMAN. Yes. Well, I couldn't think of any other way.

TESMAN (*stands in front of her*). Auntie Juju, have you gone completely out of your mind? That annuity's all you and Auntie Rena have.

MISS TESMAN. All right, there's no need to get so excited about it. It's a pure formality, you know. Judge Brack told me so. He was so kind as to arrange it all for me. A pure formality; those were his very words.

TESMAN. I dare say. All the same –

MISS TESMAN. Anyway, you'll have a salary of your own now. And, good heavens, even if we did have to fork out a little – tighten our belts for a week or two – why, we'd be happy to do so for your sake.

TESMAN. Oh, Auntie Juju! Will you never stop sacrificing yourself for me?

MISS TESMAN (*gets up and puts her hands on his shoulders*). What else have I to live for but to smooth your road a little, my dear boy? You've never had any mother or father to turn to. And now at last we've achieved our goal. I won't deny we've had our little difficulties now and then. But now, thank the good Lord, George dear, all your worries are past.

TESMAN. Yes, it's wonderful really how everything's gone just right for me.

MISS TESMAN. Yes! And the enemies who tried to bar your way have been struck down. They have been made to bite the dust. The man who was your most dangerous rival has had the mightiest fall. And now he's lying there in the pit he dug for himself, poor misguided creature.

TESMAN. Have you heard any news of Eilert? Since I went away?

MISS TESMAN. Only that he's said to have published a new book.

TESMAN. What! Eilert Loevborg? You mean – just recently? What?

MISS TESMAN. So they say. I don't imagine it can be of any value, do you? When your new book comes out, that'll be another story. What's it going to be about?

TESMAN. The domestic industries of Brabant in the Middle Ages.

MISS TESMAN. Oh, George! The things you know about!

TESMAN. Mind you, it may be some time before I actually get down to writing it. I've made these very extensive notes, and I've got to file and index them first.

MISS TESMAN. Ah, yes! Making notes; filing and indexing; you've always been wonderful at that. Poor dear Joachim was just the same.

TESMAN. I'm looking forward so much to getting down to that. Especially now I've a home of my own to work in.

MISS TESMAN. And above all, now that you have the girl you set your heart on, George dear.

TESMAN (*embraces her*). Oh, yes, Auntie Juju, yes! Hedda's the loveliest thing of all! (*Looks towards the doorway.*) I think I hear her coming. What?

HEDDA *enters the rear room from the left, and comes into the drawing-room. She is a woman of twenty-nine. Distinguished,*

*aristocratic face and figure. Her complexion is pale and
opalescent. Her eyes are steel-grey, with an expression of cold,
calm serenity. Her hair is of a handsome auburn colour, but
is not especially abundant. She is dressed in an elegant, somewhat loose-fitting morning gown.*

MISS TESMAN (*goes to greet her*). Good morning, Hedda dear!
Good morning!

HEDDA (*holds out her hand*). Good morning, dear Miss Tesman.
What an early hour to call. So kind of you.

MISS TESMAN (*seems somewhat embarrassed*). And has the
young bride slept well in her new home?

HEDDA. Oh – thank you, yes. Passably well.

TESMAN (*laughs*). Passably? I say. Hedda, that's good! When
I jumped out of bed, you were sleeping like a top.

HEDDA. Yes. Fortunately. One has to accustom oneself to
anything new, Miss Tesman. It takes time. (*Looks left.*) Oh,
that maid's left the french windows open. This room's
flooded with sun.

MISS TESMAN (*goes towards the windows*). Oh – let me close
them.

HEDDA. No, no, don't do that. Tesman dear, draw the curtains.
This light's blinding me.

TESMAN (*at the windows*). Yes, yes, dear. There, Hedda, now
you've got shade and fresh air.

HEDDA. This room needs fresh air. All these flowers –! But my
dear Miss Tesman, won't you take a seat?

MISS TESMAN. No, really not, thank you. I just wanted to make
sure you have everything you need. I must see about getting
back home. My poor dear sister will be waiting for me.

TESMAN. Be sure to give her my love, won't you? Tell her I'll
run over and see her later today.

MISS TESMAN. Oh yes, I'll tell her that. Oh, George – (*Fumbles
in the pocket of her skirt.*) I almost forgot. I've brought
something for you.

TESMAN. What's that, Auntie Juju? What?

MISS TESMAN (*pulls out a flat package wrapped in newspaper and gives it to him*). Open and see, dear boy.

TESMAN (*opens the package*). Good heavens! Auntie Juju, you've kept them! Hedda, this is really very touching. What?

HEDDA (*by the what-nots, on the right*). What is it, Tesman?

TESMAN. My old shoes! My slippers, Hedda!

HEDDA. Oh, them. I remember you kept talking about them on our honeymoon.

TESMAN. Yes, I missed them dreadfully. (*Goes over to her.*) Here, Hedda, take a look.

HEDDA (*goes away towards the stove*). Thanks, I won't bother.

TESMAN (*follows her*). Fancy, Hedda, Auntie Rena's embroidered them for me. Despite her being so ill. Oh, you can't imagine what memories they have for me.

HEDDA (*by the table*). Not for me.

MISS TESMAN. No, Hedda's right there, George.

TESMAN. Yes, but I thought since she's one of the family now –

HEDDA (*interrupts*). Tesman, we really can't go on keeping this maid.

MISS TESMAN. Not keep Bertha?

TESMAN. What makes you say that, dear? What?

HEDDA (*points*). Look at that! She's left her old hat lying on the chair.

TESMAN (*appalled, drops his slippers on the floor*). But, Hedda –!

HEDDA. Suppose someone came in and saw it?

TESMAN. But, Hedda – that's Auntie Juju's hat.

HEDDA. Oh?

MISS TESMAN (*picks up the hat*). Indeed it's mine. And it doesn't happen to be old, Hedda dear.

HEDDA. I didn't look at it very closely, Miss Tesman.

MISS TESMAN (*tying on the hat*). As a matter of fact, it's the first time I've worn it. As the good Lord is my witness.

TESMAN. It's very pretty, too. Really smart.

MISS TESMAN. Oh, I'm afraid it's nothing much really. (*Looks round.*) My parasol. Ah, there it is. (*Takes it.*) This is mine, too. (*Murmurs.*) Not Bertha's.

TESMAN. A new hat and a new parasol! I say, Hedda, fancy that!

HEDDA. Very pretty and charming.

TESMAN. Yes, isn't it? What? But, Auntie Juju, take a good look at Hedda before you go. Isn't she pretty and charming?

MISS TESMAN. Dear boy, there's nothing new in that. Hedda's been a beauty ever since the day she was born. (*Nods and goes right.*)

TESMAN (*follows her*). Yes, but have you noticed how strong and healthy she's looking? And how she's filled out since we went away?

MISS TESMAN (*stops and turns*). Filled out?

HEDDA (*walks across the room*). Oh, can't we forget it?

TESMAN. Yes, Auntie Juju – you can't see it so clearly with that dress on. But I've good reason to know –

HEDDA (*by the french windows, impatiently*). You haven't good reason to know anything.

TESMAN. It must have been the mountain air up there in the Tyrol –

HEDDA (*curtly, interrupts him*). I'm exactly the same as when I went away.

TESMAN. You keep on saying so. But you're not. I'm right, aren't I, Auntie Juju?

MISS TESMAN (*has folded her hands and is gazing at her*). She's beautiful – beautiful. Hedda is beautiful. (*Goes over to* HEDDA, *takes her head between her hands, draws it down and kisses her hair.*) God bless and keep you, Hedda Tesman. For George's sake.

HEDDA (*frees herself politely*). Oh – let me go, please.

MISS TESMAN (*quietly, emotionally*). I shall come and see you both every day.

TESMAN. Yes, Auntie Juju, please do. What?

MISS TESMAN. Good-bye! Good-bye!

She goes out into the hall. TESMAN *follows her. The door remains open.* TESMAN *is heard sending his love to* AUNT RENA *and thanking* MISS TESMAN *for his slippers. Meanwhile* HEDDA *walks up and down the room, raising her arms and clenching her fists as though in desperation. Then she throws aside the curtains from the french windows and stands there, looking out. A few moments later* TESMAN *returns and closes the door behind him.*

TESMAN (*picks up his slippers from the floor*). What are you looking at, Hedda?

HEDDA (*calm and controlled again*). Only the leaves. They're so golden and withered.

TESMAN (*wraps up the slippers and lays them on the table*). Well, we're in September now.

HEDDA (*restless again*). Yes. We're already into September.

TESMAN. Auntie Juju was behaving rather oddly, I thought, didn't you? Almost as though she was in church or something. I wonder what came over her. Any idea?

HEDDA. I hardly know her. Does she often act like that?

TESMAN. Not to the extent she did today.

HEDDA (*goes away from the french windows*). Do you think she was hurt by what I said about the hat?

TESMAN. Oh, I don't think so. A little at first, perhaps –

HEDDA. But what a thing to do, throw her hat down in someone's drawing-room. People don't do such things.

TESMAN. I'm sure Auntie Juju doesn't do it very often.

HEDDA. Oh well, I'll make it up with her.

TESMAN. Oh Hedda, would you?

HEDDA. When you see them this afternoon invite her to come out here this evening.

TESMAN. You bet I will! I say, there's another thing which would please her enormously.

HEDDA. Oh?

TESMAN. If you could bring yourself to call her Auntie Juju. For my sake, Hedda? What?

HEDDA. Oh no, really, Tesman, you mustn't ask me to do that. I've told you so once before. I'll try to call her Aunt Juliana. That's as far as I'll go.

TESMAN (*after a moment*). I say, Hedda, is anything wrong? What?

HEDDA. I'm just looking at my old piano. It doesn't really go with all this.

TESMAN. As soon as I start getting my salary we'll see about changing it.

HEDDA. No, no, don't let's change it. I don't want to part with it. We can move it into that little room and get another one to put in here.

TESMAN (*a little downcast*). Yes, we – might do that.

HEDDA (*picks up the bunch of flowers from the piano*). These flowers weren't here when we arrived last night.

TESMAN. I expect Auntie Juju brought them.

HEDDA. Here's a card. (*Takes it out and reads.*) 'Will come back later today.' Guess who it's from?

TESMAN. No idea. Who? What?

HEDDA. It says: 'Mrs Elvsted.'

TESMAN. No, really? Mrs Elvsted! She used to be Miss Rysing, didn't she?

HEDDA. Yes. She was the one with that irritating hair she was always showing off. I hear she used to be an old flame of yours.

TESMAN (*laughs*). That didn't last long. Anyway, that was before I got to know you, Hedda. By Jove, fancy her being in town!

HEDDA. Strange she should call. I only knew her at school.

TESMAN. Yes, I haven't seen her for – oh, heaven knows how long. I don't know how she manages to stick it out up there in the north. What?

HEDDA (*thinks for a moment, then says suddenly*). Tell me, Tesman, doesn't he live somewhere up in those parts? You know – Eilert Loevborg?

TESMAN. Yes, that's right. So he does.

BERTHA *enters from the hall.*

BERTHA. She's here again, madam. The lady who came and left the flowers. (*Points.*) The ones you're holding.

HEDDA. Oh, is she? Well, show her in.

BERTHA *opens the door for* MRS ELVSTED *and goes out.* MRS ELVSTED *is a delicately built woman with gentle, attractive features. Her eyes are light blue, large, and somewhat prominent, with a frightened, questioning expression. Her hair is extremely fair, almost flaxen, and is exceptionally wavy and abundant. She is two or three years younger than* HEDDA. *She is wearing a dark visiting dress, in good taste but not quite in the latest fashion.*

(*Goes cordially to greet her.*) Dear Mrs Elvsted, good morning! How delightful to see you again after all this time!

MRS ELVSTED (*nervously, trying to control herself*). Yes, it's many years since we met.

TESMAN. And since *we* met. What?

HEDDA. Thank you for your lovely flowers.

MRS ELVSTED. I wanted to come yesterday afternoon. But they told me you were away –

TESMAN. You've only just arrived in town, then? What?

MRS ELVSTED. I got here yesterday, around midday. Oh, I became almost desperate when I heard you weren't here.

HEDDA. Desperate? Why?

TESMAN. My dear Mrs Rysing – Elvsted –

HEDDA. There's nothing wrong, I hope?

MRS ELVSTED. Yes, there is. And I don't know anyone else here whom I can turn to.

HEDDA (*puts the flowers down on the table*). Come and sit with me on the sofa –

MRS ELVSTED. Oh, I feel too restless to sit down.

HEDDA. You must. Come along, now.

> *She pulls* MRS ELVSTED *down on to the sofa and sits beside her.*

TESMAN. Well? Tell us, Mrs – er –

HEDDA. Has something happened at home?

MRS ELVSTED. Yes – that is, yes and no. Oh, I do hope you won't misunderstand me –

HEDDA. Then you'd better tell us the whole story, Mrs Elvsted.

TESMAN. That's why you've come. What?

MRS ELVSTED. Yes – yes, it is. Well, then – in case you don't already know – Eilert Loevborg is in town.

HEDDA. Loevborg here?

TESMAN. Eilert back in town? Fancy, Hedda, did you hear that?

HEDDA. Yes, of course I heard.

MRS ELVSTED. He's been here a week. A whole week! In this city. Alone. With all those dreadful people –

HEDDA. But, my dear Mrs Elvsted, what concern is he of yours?

MRS ELVSTED (*gives her a frightened look and says quickly*). He's been tutoring the children.

HEDDA. Your children?

MRS ELVSTED. My husband's. I have none.

HEDDA. Oh, you mean your stepchildren.

MRS ELVSTED. Yes.

TESMAN (*gropingly*). But was he sufficiently – I don't know how to put it – sufficiently regular in his habits to be suited to such a post? What?

MRS ELVSTED. For the past two to three years he has been living irreproachably.

TESMAN. You don't say! Hedda, do you hear that?

HEDDA. I hear.

MRS ELVSTED. Quite irreproachably, I assure you. In every

respect. All the same – in this big city – with money in his pockets – I'm so dreadfully frightened something may happen to him.

TESMAN. But why didn't he stay up there with you and your husband?

MRS ELVSTED. Once his book had come out, he became restless.

TESMAN. Oh, yes – Auntie Juju said he's brought out a new book.

MRS ELVSTED. Yes, a big new book about the history of civilization. A kind of general survey. It came out a fortnight ago. Everyone's been buying it and reading it – it's created a tremendous stir –

TESMAN. Has it really? It must be something he's dug up, then.

MRS ELVSTED. You mean from the old days?

TESMAN. Yes.

MRS ELVSTED. No, he's written it all since he came to live with us.

TESMAN. Well, that's splendid news, Hedda. Fancy that!

MRS ELVSTED. Oh, yes! If only he can go on like this!

HEDDA. Have you met him since you came here?

MRS ELVSTED. No, not yet. I had such dreadful difficulty finding his address. But this morning I managed to track him down at last.

HEDDA (*looks searchingly at her*). I must say I find it a little strange that your husband – hm –

MRS ELVSTED (*starts nervously*). My husband! What do you mean?

HEDDA. That he should send you all the way here on an errand of this kind. I'm surprised he didn't come himself to keep an eye on his friend.

MRS ELVSTED. Oh, no, no – my husband hasn't the time. Besides, I – er – wanted to do some shopping here.

HEDDA (*with a slight smile*). Ah. Well, that's different.

MRS ELVSTED (*gets up quickly, restlessly*). Please, Mr Tesman, I beg you – be kind to Eilert Loevborg if he comes here. I'm sure he will. I mean, you used to be such good friends in the old days. And you're both studying the same subject, as far as I can understand. You're in the same field, aren't you?

TESMAN. Well, we used to be, anyway.

MRS ELVSTED. Yes – so I beg you earnestly, do please, please, keep an eye on him. Oh, Mr Tesman, do promise me you will.

TESMAN. I shall be only too happy to do so, Mrs Rysing.

HEDDA. Elvsted.

TESMAN. I'll do everything for Eilert that lies in my power. You can rely on that.

MRS ELVSTED. Oh, how good and kind you are! (*Presses his hands.*) Thank you, thank you, thank you. (*Frightened.*) My husband's so fond of him, you see.

HEDDA (*gets up*). You'd better send him a note, Tesman. He may not come to you of his own accord.

TESMAN. Yes, that'd probably be the best plan, Hedda. What?

HEDDA. The sooner the better. Why not do it now?

MRS ELVSTED (*pleadingly*). Oh yes, if only you would!

TESMAN. I'll do it this very moment. Do you have his address, Mrs – er – Elvsted?

MRS ELVSTED. Yes. (*Takes a small piece of paper from her pocket and gives it to him.*)

TESMAN. Good, good. Right, well, I'll go inside and – (*Looks round.*) Where are my slippers? Oh yes, here. (*Picks up the package and is about to go.*)

HEDDA. Try to sound friendly. Make it a nice long letter.

TESMAN. Right, I will.

MRS ELVSTED. Please don't say anything about my having seen you.

TESMAN. Good heavens, no, of course not. What?

He goes out through the rear room to the right.

HEDDA (*goes over to* MRS ELVSTED, *smiles, and says softly*).
  Well! Now we've killed two birds with one stone.

MRS ELVSTED. What do you mean?

HEDDA. Didn't you realize I wanted to get him out of the
  room?

MRS ELVSTED. So that he could write the letter?

HEDDA. And so that I could talk to you alone.

MRS ELVSTED (*confused*). About this?

HEDDA. Yes, about this.

MRS ELVSTED (*in alarm*). But there's nothing more to tell, Mrs
  Tesman. Really there isn't.

HEDDA. Oh, yes, there is. There's a lot more. I can see that.
  Come along, let's sit down and have a little chat.

She pushes MRS ELVSTED *down into the armchair by the
stove and seats herself on one of the footstools.*

MRS ELVSTED (*looks anxiously at her watch*). Really, Mrs Tesman, I think I ought to be going now.

HEDDA. There's no hurry. Well? How are things at home?

MRS ELVSTED. I'd rather not speak about that.

HEDDA. But, my dear, you can tell me. Good heavens, we were
  at school together.

MRS ELVSTED. Yes, but you were a year senior to me. Oh, I
  used to be terribly frightened of you in those days.

HEDDA. Frightened of me?

MRS ELVSTED. Yes, terribly frightened. Whenever you met me
  on the staircase you used to pull my hair.

HEDDA. No, did I?

MRS ELVSTED. Yes. And once you said you'd burn it all
  off.

HEDDA. Oh, that was only in fun.

MRS ELVSTED. Yes, but I was so silly in those days. And then
  afterwards – I mean, we've drifted so far apart. Our back-
  grounds were so different.

HEDDA. Well, now we must try to drift together again. Now listen. When we were at school we used to call each other by our Christian names –

MRS ELVSTED. No, I'm sure you're mistaken.

HEDDA. I'm sure I'm not. I remember it quite clearly. Let's tell each other our secrets, as we used to in the old days. (*Moves closer on her footstool.*) There, now. (*Kisses her on the cheek.*) You must call me Hedda.

MRS ELVSTED (*squeezes her hands and pats them*). Oh, you're so kind. I'm not used to people being so nice to me.

HEDDA. Now, now, now. And I shall call you Tora, the way I used to.

MRS ELVSTED. My name is Thea.

HEDDA. Yes, of course. Of course. I meant Thea. (*Looks at her sympathetically.*) So you're not used to kindness, Thea? In your own home?

MRS ELVSTED. Oh, if only I had a home! But I haven't. I've never had one.

HEDDA (*looks at her for a moment*). I thought that was it.

MRS ELVSTED (*stares blankly and helplessly*). Yes – yes – yes.

HEDDA. I can't remember exactly, but didn't you first go to Mr Elvsted as a housekeeper?

MRS ELVSTED. Governess, actually. But his wife – at the time, I mean – she was an invalid, and had to spend most of her time in bed. So I had to look after the house, too.

HEDDA. But in the end, you became mistress of the house.

MRS ELVSTED (*sadly*). Yes, I did.

HEDDA. Let me see. Roughly how long ago was that?

MRS ELVSTED. When I got married, you mean?

HEDDA. Yes.

MRS ELVSTED. About five years.

HEDDA. Yes; it must be about that.

MRS ELVSTED. Oh, those five years! Especially the last two or three. Oh, Mrs Tesman, if you only knew – !

HEDDA (*slaps her hand gently*). Mrs Tesman? Oh, Thea!

MRS ELVSTED. I'm sorry, I'll try to remember. Yes – if you
    had any idea –

HEDDA (*casually*). Eilert Loevborg's been up there, too, for
    about three years, hasn't he?

MRS ELVSTED (*looks at her uncertainly*). Eilert Loevborg? Yes,
    he has.

HEDDA. Did you know him before? When you were here?

MRS ELVSTED. No, not really. That is – I knew him by name,
    of course.

HEDDA. But up there, he used to visit you?

MRS ELVSTED. Yes, he used to come and see us every day. To
    give the children lessons. I found I couldn't do that as well
    as manage the house.

HEDDA. I'm sure you couldn't. And your husband –? I suppose
    being a magistrate he has to be away from home a good
    deal?

MRS ELVSTED. Yes. You see, Mrs – you see, Hedda, he has to
    cover the whole district.

HEDDA (*leans against the arm of* MRS ELVSTED'S *chair*). Poor,
    pretty little Thea! Now you must tell me the whole story.
    From beginning to end.

MRS ELVSTED. Well – what do you want to know?

HEDDA. What kind of a man is your husband, Thea? I mean,
    as a person. Is he kind to you?

MRS ELVSTED (*evasively*). I'm sure he does his best to be.

HEDDA. I only wonder if he isn't too old for you. There's
    more than twenty years between you, isn't there?

MRS ELVSTED (*irritably*). Yes, there's that, too. Oh, there are
    so many things. We're different in every way. We've nothing
    in common. Nothing whatever.

HEDDA. But he loves you, surely? In his own way?

MRS ELVSTED. Oh, I don't know. I think he just finds me use-
    ful. And then I don't cost much to keep. I'm cheap.

HEDDA. Now you're being stupid.

MRS ELVSTED (*shakes her head*). It can't be any different. With

him. He doesn't love anyone except himself. And perhaps
the children – a little.

HEDDA. He must be fond of Eilert Loevborg, Thea.

MRS ELVSTED (*looks at her*). Eilert Loevborg? What makes you
think that?

HEDDA. Well, if he sends you all the way down here to look
for him – (*Smiles almost imperceptibly.*) Besides, you said so
yourself to Tesman.

MRS ELVSTED (*with a nervous twitch*). Did I? Oh yes, I suppose
I did. (*Impulsively, but keeping her voice low.*) Well, I might
as well tell you the whole story. It's bound to come out
sooner or later.

HEDDA. But, my dear Thea—?

MRS ELVSTED. My husband had no idea I was coming here.

HEDDA. What? Your husband didn't know?

MRS ELVSTED. No, of course not. As a matter of fact, he wasn't
even there. He was away at the assizes. Oh, I couldn't stand
it any longer, Hedda! I just couldn't. I'd be so dreadfully
lonely up there now.

HEDDA. Go on.

MRS ELVSTED. So I packed a few things. Secretly. And went.

HEDDA. Without telling anyone?

MRS ELVSTED. Yes. I caught the train and came straight here.

HEDDA. But, my dear Thea! How brave of you!

MRS ELVSTED (*gets up and walks across the room*). Well, what
else could I do?

HEDDA. But what do you suppose your husband will say when
you get back?

MRS ELVSTED (*by the table, looks at her*). Back there? To him?

HEDDA. Yes. Surely – ?

MRS ELVSTED. I shall never go back to him.

HEDDA (*gets up and goes closer*). You mean you've left your
home for good?

MRS ELVSTED. Yes. I didn't see what else I could do.

HEDDA. But to do it so openly!

MRS ELVSTED. Oh, it's no use trying to keep a thing like that secret.

HEDDA. But what do you suppose people will say?

MRS ELVSTED. They can say what they like. (*Sits sadly, wearily on the sofa.*) I had to do it.

HEDDA (*after a short silence*). What do you intend to do now? How are you going to live?

MRS ELVSTED. I don't know. I only know that I must live wherever Eilert Loevborg is. If I am to go on living.

HEDDA (*moves a chair from the table, sits on it near* MRS ELVSTED *and strokes her hands*). Tell me, Thea, how did this – friendship between you and Eilert Loevborg begin?

MRS ELVSTED. Oh, it came about gradually. I developed a kind of – power over him.

HEDDA. Oh?

MRS ELVSTED. He gave up his old habits. Not because I asked him to. I'd never have dared to do that. I suppose he just noticed I didn't like that kind of thing. So he gave it up.

HEDDA (*hides a smile*). So you've made a new man of him! Clever little Thea!

MRS ELVSTED. Yes – anyway, he says I have. And he's made a – sort of – real person of me. Taught me to think – and to understand all kinds of things.

HEDDA. Did he give you lessons, too?

MRS ELVSTED. Not exactly lessons. But he talked to me. About – oh, you've no idea – so many things! And then he let me work with him. Oh, it was wonderful. I was so happy to be allowed to help him.

HEDDA. Did he allow you to help him?

MRS ELVSTED. Yes. Whenever he wrote anything we always – did it together.

HEDDA. Like good friends?

MRS ELVSTED (*eagerly*). Friends! Yes – why, Hedda that's exactly the word he used! Oh, I ought to feel so happy. But I can't. I don't know if it will last.

HEDDA. You don't seem very sure of him.

MRS ELVSTED (*sadly*). Something stands between Eilert Loevborg and me. The shadow of another woman.

HEDDA. Who can that be?

MRS ELVSTED. I don't know. Someone he used to be friendly with in – in the old days. Someone he's never been able to forget.

HEDDA. What has he told you about her?

MRS ELVSTED. Oh, he only mentioned her once, casually.

HEDDA. Well! What did he say?

MRS ELVSTED. He said when he left her she tried to shoot him with a pistol.

HEDDA (*cold, controlled*). What nonsense. People don't do such things. The kind of people we know.

MRS ELVSTED. No. I think it must have been that red-haired singer he used to –

HEDDA. Ah yes, very probably.

MRS ELVSTED. I remember they used to say she always carried a loaded pistol.

HEDDA. Well then, it must be her.

MRS ELVSTED. But, Hedda, I hear she's come back, and is living here. Oh, I'm so desperate – !

HEDDA (*glances towards the rear room*). Ssh! Tesman's coming. (*Gets up and whispers.*) Thea, we mustn't breathe a word about this to anyone.

MRS ELVSTED (*jumps up*). Oh, no, no! Please don't!

> GEORGE TESMAN *appears from the right in the rear room with a letter in his hand, and comes into the drawing-room.*

TESMAN. Well, here's my little epistle all signed and sealed.

HEDDA. Good. I think Mrs Elvsted wants to go now. Wait a moment – I'll see you as far as the garden gate.

TESMAN. Er – Hedda, do you think Bertha could deal with this?

HEDDA (*takes the letter*). I'll give her instructions.

BERTHA *enters from the hall.*

BERTHA. Judge Brack is here and asks if he may pay his respects to madam and the Doctor.

HEDDA. Yes, ask him to be so good as to come in. And – wait a moment – drop this letter in the post box.

BERTHA *(takes the letter).* Very good, madam.

> *She opens the door for* JUDGE BRACK, *and goes out.* JUDGE BRACK *is forty-five; rather short, but well built, and elastic in his movements. He has a roundish face with an aristocratic profile. His hair, cut short, is still almost black, and is carefully barbered. Eyes lively and humorous. Thick eyebrows. His moustache is also thick, and is trimmed square at the ends. He is wearing outdoor clothes which are elegant but a little too youthful for him. He has a monocle in one eye; now and then he lets it drop.*

BRACK *(hat in hand, bows).* May one presume to call so early?

HEDDA. One may presume.

TESMAN *(shakes his hand).* You're welcome here any time. Judge Brack – Mrs Rysing.

> HEDDA *sighs.*

BRACK *(bows).* Ah – charmed –

HEDDA *(looks at him and laughs).* What fun to be able to see you by daylight for once, Judge.

BRACK. Do I look – different?

HEDDA. Yes. A little younger, I think.

BRACK. Too kind.

TESMAN. Well, what do you think of Hedda? What? Doesn't she look well? Hasn't she filled out – ?

HEDDA. Oh, do stop it. You ought to be thanking Judge Brack for all the inconvenience he's put himself to –

BRACK. Nonsense, it was a pleasure –

HEDDA. You're a loyal friend. But my other friend is pining to get away, Au revoir, Judge. I won't be a minute.

Mutual salutations. MRS ELVSTED *and* HEDDA *go out through the hall.*

BRACK. Well, is your wife satisfied with everything?

TESMAN. Yes, we can't thank you enough. That is – we may have to shift one or two things around, she tells me. And we're short of one or two little items we'll have to purchase.

BRACK. Oh? Really?

TESMAN. But you mustn't worry your head about that. Hedda says she'll get what's needed. I say, why don't we sit down? What?

BRACK. Thanks, just for a moment. (*Sits at the table.*) There's something I'd like to talk to you about, my dear Tesman.

TESMAN. Oh? Ah yes, of course. (*Sits.*) After the feast comes the reckoning. What?

BRACK. Oh, never mind about the financial side – there's no hurry about that. Though I could wish we'd arranged things a little less palatially.

TESMAN. Good heavens, that'd never have done. Think of Hedda, my dear chap. You know her. I couldn't possibly ask her to live like a petty bourgeois.

BRACK. No, no – that's just the problem.

TESMAN. Anyway, it can't be long now before my nomination comes through.

BRACK. Well, you know, these things often take time.

TESMAN. Have you heard any more news? What?

BRACK. Nothing definite. (*Changing the subject.*) Oh, by the way, I have one piece of news for you.

TESMAN. What?

BRACK. Your old friend Eilert Loevborg is back in town.

TESMAN. I know that already.

BRACK. Oh? How did you hear that?

TESMAN. She told me. That lady who went out with Hedda.

BRACK. I see. What was her name? I didn't catch it.

TESMAN. Mrs Elvsted.

BRACK. Oh, the magistrate's wife. Yes, Loevborg's been living up near them, hasn't he?

TESMAN. I'm delighted to hear he's become a decent human being again.

BRACK. Yes, so they say.

TESMAN. I gather he's published a new book, too. What?

BRACK. Indeed he has.

TESMAN. I hear it's created rather a stir.

BRACK. Quite an unusual stir.

TESMAN. I say, isn't that splendid news! He's such a gifted chap – and I was afraid he'd gone to the dogs for good.

BRACK. Most people thought he had.

TESMAN. But I can't think what he'll do now. How on earth will he manage to make ends meet? What?

As he speaks his last words HEDDA *enters from the hall.*

HEDDA (*to* BRACK, *laughs slightly scornfully*). Tesman is always worrying about making ends meet.

TESMAN. We were talking about poor Eilert Loevborg, Hedda dear.

HEDDA (*gives him a quick look*). Oh, were you? (*Sits in the armchair by the stove and asks casually.*) Is he in trouble?

TESMAN. Well, he must have run through his inheritance long ago by now. And he can't write a new book every year. What? So I'm wondering what's going to become of him.

BRACK. I may be able to enlighten you there.

TESMAN. Oh?

BRACK. You mustn't forget he has relatives who wield a good deal of influence.

TESMAN. Relatives? Oh, they've quite washed their hands of him, I'm afraid.

BRACK. They used to regard him as the hope of the family.

TESMAN. Used to, yes. But he's put an end to that.

HEDDA. Who knows? (*With a little smile.*) I hear the Elvsteds have made a new man of him.

BRACK. And then this book he's just published –

TESMAN. Well, let's hope they find something for him. I've just written him a note. Oh, by the way, Hedda, I asked him to come over and see us this evening.

BRACK. But, my dear chap, you're coming to me this evening. My bachelor party. You promised me last night when I met you at the boat.

HEDDA. Had you forgotten, Tesman?

TESMAN. Good heavens, yes, I'd quite forgotten.

BRACK. Anyway, you can be quite sure he won't turn up here.

TESMAN. Why do you think that? What?

BRACK (*a little unwillingly, gets up and rests his hands on the back of his chair*). My dear Tesman – and you, too, Mrs Tesman – there's something I feel you ought to know.

TESMAN. Concerning Eilert?

BRACK. Concerning him and you.

TESMAN Well, my dear Judge, tell us, please!

BRACK. You must be prepared for your nomination not to come through quite as quickly as you hope and expect.

TESMAN (*jumps up uneasily*). Is anything wrong? What?

BRACK. There's a possibility that the appointment may be decided by competition –

TESMAN. Competition! Hedda, fancy that!

HEDDA (*leans further back in her chair*). Ah! How interesting!

TESMAN. But who else – ? I say, you don't mean – ?

BRACK. Exactly. By competition with Eilert Loevborg.

TESMAN (*clasps his hands in alarm*). No, no, but this is inconceivable! It's absolutely impossible! What?

BRACK. Hm. We may find it'll happen, all the same.

TESMAN. No, but – Judge Brack, they couldn't be so inconsiderate towards me! (*Waves his arms.*) I mean, by Jove, I – I'm a married man! It was on the strength of this that Hedda and I *got* married! We've run up some pretty hefty debts. And borrowed money from Auntie Juju! I mean, good heavens, they practically promised me the appointment. What?

BRACK. Well, well, I'm sure you'll get it. But you'll have to go through a competition.

HEDDA (*motionless in her armchair*). How exciting, Tesman. It'll be a kind of duel, by Jove.

TESMAN. My dear Hedda, how can you take it so lightly?

HEDDA (*as before*). I'm not. I can't wait to see who's going to win.

BRACK. In any case, Mrs Tesman, it's best you should know how things stand. I mean before you commit yourself to these little items I hear you're threatening to purchase.

HEDDA. I can't allow this to alter my plans.

BRACK. Indeed? Well, that's your business. Good-bye. (*To* TESMAN.) I'll come and collect you on the way home from my afternoon walk.

TESMAN. Oh, yes, yes. I'm sorry, I'm all upside down just now.

HEDDA (*lying in her chair, holds out her hand*). Good-bye, Judge. See you this afternoon.

BRACK. Thank you. Good-bye, good-bye.

TESMAN (*sees him to the door*): Good-bye, my dear Judge. You will excuse me, won't you?

JUDGE BRACK *goes out through the hall.*

(*Pacing up and down*). Oh, Hedda! One oughtn't to go plunging off on wild adventures. What?

HEDDA (*looks at him and smiles*). Like you're doing?

TESMAN. Yes. I mean, there's no denying it, it was a pretty big adventure to go off and get married and set up house merely on expectation.

HEDDA. Perhaps you're right.

TESMAN. Well, anyway, we have our home, Hedda. My word, yes! The home we dreamed of. And set our hearts on. What?

HEDDA (*gets up slowly, wearily*). You agreed that we should enter society. And keep open house. That was the bargain.

TESMAN. Yes. Good heavens, I was looking forward to it all so much. To seeing you play hostess to a select circle! By Jove! What? Ah, well, for the time being we.shall have to make do with each other's company, Hedda. Perhaps have Auntie Juju in now and then. Oh dear, this wasn't at all what you had in mind –

HEDDA. I won't be able to have a liveried footman. For a start.

TESMAN. Oh no, we couldn't possibly afford a footman.

HEDDA. And the bay mare you promised me –

TESMAN (*fearfully*). Bay mare!

HEDDA. I mustn't even think of that now.

TESMAN. Heaven forbid!

HEDDA (*walks across the room*). Ah, well. I still have one thing left to amuse myself with.

TESMAN (*joyfully*). Thank goodness for that. What's that, Hedda? What?

HEDDA (*in the open doorway, looks at him with concealed scorn*). My pistols, George darling.

TESMAN (*alarmed*). Pistols!

HEDDA (*her eyes cold*). General Gabler's pistols.

She goes into the rear room and disappears.

TESMAN (*runs to the doorway and calls after her*). For heaven's sake, Hedda dear, don't touch those things. They're dangerous. Hedda – please – for my sake! What?

Act Two

The same as in Act One, except that the piano has been removed and an elegant little writing-table, with a bookcase, stands in its place. By the sofa on the left a smaller table has been placed. Most of the flowers have been removed. MRS ELVSTED'S *bouquet stands on the larger table, downstage. It is afternoon.*

HEDDA, *dressed to receive callers, is alone in the room. She is standing by the open french windows, loading a revolver. The pair to it is lying in an open pistol-case on the writing-table.*

HEDDA (*looks down into the garden and calls*). Good afternoon, Judge.

BRACK (*in the distance, below*). Afternoon, Mrs Tesman.

HEDDA (*raises the pistol and takes aim*). I'm going to shoot you, Judge Brack.

BRACK (*shouts from below*). No, no, no! Don't aim that thing at me!

HEDDA. This'll teach you to enter houses by the back door.

She fires.

BRACK (*below*). Have you gone completely out of your mind?

HEDDA. Oh dear! Did I hit you?

BRACK (*still outside*). Stop playing these silly tricks.

HEDDA. All right, Judge. Come along in.

JUDGE BRACK, *dressed for a bachelor party, enters through the french windows. He has a light overcoat on his arm.*

BRACK. For God's sake, haven't you stopped fooling around with those things yet? What are you trying to hit?

HEDDA. Oh, I was just shooting at the sky.

BRACK (*takes the pistol gently from her hand*). By your leave, ma'am. (*Looks at it.*) Ah, yes – I know this old friend well.

(*Looks around.*) Where's the case? Oh, yes. (*Puts the pistol in the case and closes it.*) That's enough of that little game for today.

HEDDA. Well, what on earth *am* I to do?

BRACK. You haven't had any visitors?

HEDDA (*closes the french windows*). Not one. I suppose the best people are all still in the country.

BRACK. Your husband isn't home yet?

HEDDA (*locks the pistol away in a drawer of the writing-table*). No. The moment he'd finished eating he ran off to his aunties. He wasn't expecting you so early.

BRACK. Ah, why didn't I think of that? How stupid of me.

HEDDA (*turns her head and looks at him*). Why stupid?

BRACK. I'd have come a little sooner.

HEDDA (*walks across the room*). There'd have been no one to receive you. I've been in my room since lunch, dressing.

BRACK. You haven't a tiny crack in the door through which we might have negotiated?

HEDDA. You forgot to arrange one.

BRACK. Another stupidity.

HEDDA. Well, we'll have to sit down here. And wait. Tesman won't be back for some time.

BRACK. Sad. Well, I'll be patient.

> HEDDA *sits on the corner of the sofa.* BRACK *puts his coat over the back of the nearest chair and seats himself, keeping his hat in his hand. Short pause. They look at each other.*

HEDDA. Well?

BRACK (*in the same tone of voice*). Well?

HEDDA. I asked first.

BRACK (*leans forward slightly*). Yes, well, now we can enjoy a nice, cosy little chat – Mrs Hedda.

HEDDA (*leans further back in her chair*). It seems ages since we had a talk. I don't count last night or this morning.

BRACK. You mean: *à deux?*

HEDDA. Mm – yes. That's roughly what I meant.

BRACK. I've been longing so much for you to come home.

HEDDA. So have I.

BRACK. You? Really, Mrs Hedda? And I thought you were having such a wonderful honeymoon.

HEDDA. Oh, yes. Wonderful!

BRACK. But your husband wrote such ecstatic letters.

HEDDA. He! Oh, yes! He thinks life has nothing better to offer than rooting around in libraries and copying old pieces of parchment, or whatever it is he does.

BRACK (*a little maliciously*). Well, that *is* his life. Most of it, anyway.

HEDDA. Yes, I know. Well, it's all right for him. But for me! Oh no, my dear Judge. I've been bored to death.

BRACK (*sympathetically*). Do you mean that? Seriously?

HEDDA. Yes. Can you imagine? Six whole months without ever meeting a single person who was one of us, and to whom I could talk about the kind of things we talk about.

BRACK. Yes, I can understand. I'd miss that, too.

HEDDA. That wasn't the worst, though.

BRACK. What was?

HEDDA. Having to spend every minute of one's life with – with the same person.

BRACK (*nods*). Yes. What a thought! Morning; noon; and –

HEDDA (*coldly*). As I said: every minute of one's life.

BRACK. I stand corrected. But dear Tesman is such a clever fellow, I should have thought one ought to be able –

HEDDA. Tesman is only interested in one thing, my dear Judge. His special subject.

BRACK. True.

HEDDA. And people who are only interested in one thing don't make the most amusing company. Not for long, anyway.

BRACK. Not even when they happen to be the person one loves?

HEDDA. Oh, don't use that sickly, stupid word.

BRACK (*starts*). But, Mrs Hedda – !

HEDDA (*half laughing, half annoyed*). You just try it, Judge.
Listening to the history of civilization morning, noon and –

BRACK (*corrects her*). Every minute of one's life.

HEDDA. All right. Oh, and those domestic industries of Brabant
in the Middle Ages! That really is beyond the limit.

BRACK (*looks at her searchingly*). But, tell me – if you feel like
this why on earth did you – ? Hm –

HEDDA. Why on earth did I marry George Tesman?

BRACK. If you like to put it that way.

HEDDA. Do you think it so very strange?

BRACK. Yes – and no, Mrs Hedda.

HEDDA. I'd danced myself tired, Judge. I felt my time was
up – (*Gives a slight shudder.*) No, I mustn't say that. Or even
think it.

BRACK. You've no rational cause to think it.

HEDDA. Oh – cause, cause – (*Looks searchingly at him.*) After
all, George Tesman – well, I mean, he's a very respectable
man.

BRACK. Very respectable, sound as a rock. No denying that.

HEDDA. And there's nothing exactly ridiculous about him. Is
there?

BRACK. Ridiculous? N-no, I wouldn't say that.

HEDDA. Mm. He's very clever at collecting material and all
that, isn't he? I mean, he may go quite far in time.

BRACK (*looks at her a little uncertainly*). I thought you believed,
like everyone else, that he would become a very prominent
man.

HEDDA (*looks tired*). Yes, I did. And when he came and begged
me on his bended knees to be allowed to love and to cherish
me, I didn't see why I shouldn't let him.

BRACK. No, well – if one looks at it like that –

HEDDA. It was more than my other admirers were prepared to
do, Judge dear.

BRACK (*laughs*). Well, I can't answer for the others. As far as I myself am concerned, you know I've always had a considerable respect for the institution of marriage. As an institution.

HEDDA (*lightly*). Oh, I've never entertained any hopes of you.

BRACK. All I want is to have a circle of friends whom I can trust, whom I can help with advice or – or by any other means, and into whose houses I may come and go as a – trusted friend.

HEDDA. Of the husband?

BRACK (*bows*). Preferably, to be frank, of the wife. And of the husband too, of course. Yes, you know, this kind of triangle is a delightful arrangement for all parties concerned.

HEDDA. Yes, I often longed for a third person while I was away. Oh, those hours we spent alone in railway compartments –

BRACK. Fortunately your honeymoon is now over.

HEDDA (*shakes her head*). There's a long, long way still to go. I've only reached a stop on the line.

BRACK. Why not jump out and stretch your legs a little, Mrs Hedda?

HEDDA. I'm not the jumping sort.

BRACK. Aren't you?

HEDDA. No. There's always someone around who –

BRACK (*laughs*). Who looks at one's legs?

HEDDA. Yes. Exactly.

BRACK. Well, but surely –

HEDDA (*with a gesture of rejection*). I don't like it. I'd rather stay where I am. Sitting in the compartment. *À deux.*

BRACK. But suppose a third person were to step into the compartment?

HEDDA. That would be different.

BRACK. A trusted friend – someone who understood –

HEDDA. And was lively and amusing –

BRACK. And interested in – more subjects than one –

HEDDA (*sighs audibly*). Yes, that'd be a relief.

BRACK (*hears the front door open and shut*). The triangle is completed.

HEDDA (*half under her breath*). And the train goes on.

> GEORGE TESMAN, *in grey walking dress with a soft felt hat, enters from the hall. He has a number of paper-covered books under his arm and in his pockets.*

TESMAN (*goes over to the table by the corner sofa*). Phew! It's too hot to be lugging all this around. (*Puts the books down.*) I'm positively sweating, Hedda. Why, hullo, hullo! You here already, Judge? What? Bertha didn't tell me.

BRACK (*gets up*). I came in through the garden.

HEDDA. What are all those books you've got there?

TESMAN (*stands glancing through them*). Oh, some new publications dealing with my special subject. I had to buy them.

HEDDA. Your special subject?

BRACK. His special subject, Mrs Tesman.

> BRACK *and* HEDDA *exchange a smile.*

HEDDA. Haven't you collected enough material on your special subject?

TESMAN. My dear Hedda, one can never have too much. One must keep abreast of what other people are writing.

HEDDA. Yes. Of course.

TESMAN (*rooting among the books*). Look – I bought a copy of Eilert Loevborg's new book, too. (*Holds it out to her.*) Perhaps you'd like to have a look at it, Hedda? What?

HEDDA. No, thank you. Er – yes, perhaps I will, later.

TESMAN. I glanced through it on my way home.

BRACK. What's your opinion – as a specialist on the subject?

TESMAN. I'm amazed how sound and balanced it is. He never used to write like that. (*Gathers his books together.*) Well, I must get down to these at once. I can hardly wait to cut the pages. Oh, I've got to change, too. (*To* BRACK.) We don't have to be off just yet, do we? What?

BRACK. Heavens, no. We've plenty of time yet.

TESMAN. Good, I needn't hurry, then. (*Goes with his books, but stops and turns in the doorway.*) Oh, by the way, Hedda, Auntie Juju won't be coming to see you this evening.

HEDDA. Won't she? Oh – the hat, I suppose.

TESMAN. Good heavens, no. How could you think such a thing of Auntie Juju? Fancy –! No, Auntie Rena's very ill.

HEDDA. She always is.

TESMAN. Yes, but today she's been taken really bad.

HEDDA. Oh, then it's quite understandable that the other one should want to stay with her. Well, I shall have to swallow my disappointment.

TESMAN. You can't imagine how happy Auntie Juju was in spite of everything. At your looking so well after the honeymoon!

HEDDA (*half beneath her breath, as she rises*). Oh, these everlasting aunts!

TESMAN. What?

HEDDA (*goes over to the french windows*). Nothing.

TESMAN. Oh. All right. (*Goes into the rear room and out of sight.*)

BRACK. What was that about the hat?

HEDDA. Oh, something that happened with Miss Tesman this morning. She'd put her hat down on a chair. (*Looks at him and smiles.*) And I pretended to think it was the servant's.

BRACK (*shakes his head*). But, my dear Mrs Hedda, how could you do such a thing? To that poor old lady?

HEDDA (*nervously, walking across the room*). Sometimes a mood like that hits me. And I can't stop myself. (*Throws herself down in the armchair by the stove.*) Oh, I don't know how to explain it.

BRACK (*behind her chair*). You're not really happy. That's the answer.

HEDDA (*stares ahead of her*). Why on earth should I be happy? Can you give me a reason?

BRACK. Yes. For one thing you've got the home you always wanted.

HEDDA (*looks at him*). You really believe that story?

BRACK. You mean it isn't true?

HEDDA. Oh, yes, it's partly true.

BRACK. Well?

HEDDA. It's true I got Tesman to see me home from parties last summer –

BRACK. It was a pity my home lay in another direction.

HEDDA. Yes. Your interests lay in another direction, too.

BRACK (*laughs*). That's naughty of you, Mrs Hedda. But to return to you and George –

HEDDA. Well, we walked past this house one evening. And poor Tesman was fidgeting in his boots trying to find something to talk about. I felt sorry for the great scholar –

BRACK (*smiles incredulously*). Did you? Hm.

HEDDA. Yes, honestly I did. Well, to help him out of his misery, I happened to say quite frivolously how much I'd love to live in this house.

BRACK. Was that all?

HEDDA. That evening, yes.

BRACK. But – afterwards?

HEDDA. Yes. My little frivolity had its consequences, my dear Judge.

BRACK. Our little frivolities do. Much too often, unfortunately.

HEDDA. Thank you. Well, it was our mutual admiration for the late Prime Minister's house that brought George Tesman and me together on common ground. So we got engaged, and we got married, and we went on our honeymoon, and – Ah well, Judge, I've – made my bed and I must lie in it, I was about to say.

BRACK. How utterly fantastic! And you didn't really care in the least about the house?

HEDDA. God knows I didn't.

BRACK. Yes, but now that we've furnished it so beautifully for you?

HEDDA. Ugh – all the rooms smell of lavender and dried roses. But perhaps Auntie Juju brought that in.

BRACK (*laughs*). More likely the Prime Minister's widow, rest her soul.

HEDDA. Yes, it's got the odour of death about it. It reminds me of the flowers one has worn at a ball – the morning after. (*Clasps her hands behind her neck, leans back in the chair and looks up at him.*) Oh, my dear Judge, you've no idea how hideously bored I'm going to be out here.

BRACK. Couldn't you find some – occupation, Mrs Hedda? Like your husband?

HEDDA. Occupation? That'd interest me?

BRACK. Well – preferably.

HEDDA. God knows what. I've often thought – (*Breaks off.*) No, that wouldn't work either.

BRACK. Who knows? Tell me about it.

HEDDA. I was thinking – if I could persuade Tesman to go into politics, for example.

BRACK (*laughs*). Tesman! No, honestly, I don't think he's quite cut out to be a politician.

HEDDA. Perhaps not. But if I could persuade him to have a go at it?

BRACK. What satisfaction would that give you? If he turned out to be no good? Why do you want to make him do that?

HEDDA. Because I'm bored. (*After a moment.*) You feel there's absolutely no possibility of Tesman becoming Prime Minister, then?

BRACK. Well, you know, Mrs Hedda, for one thing he'd have to be pretty well off before he could become that.

HEDDA (*gets up impatiently*). There you are! (*Walks across the room.*) It's this wretched poverty that makes life so hateful. And ludicrous. Well, it is!

BRACK. I don't think that's the real cause.

HEDDA. What is, then?

BRACK. Nothing really exciting has ever happened to you.

HEDDA. Nothing serious, you mean?

BRACK. Call it that if you like. But now perhaps it may.

HEDDA (*tosses her head*). Oh, you're thinking of this competition for that wretched professorship? That's Tesman's affair. I'm not going to waste my time worrying about that.

BRACK. Very well, let's forget about that, then. But suppose you were to find yourself faced with what people call – to use the conventional phrase – the most solemn of human responsibilities? (*Smiles.*) A new responsibility, little Mrs Hedda.

HEDDA (*angrily*). Be quiet! Nothing like that's going to happen.

BRACK (*warily*). We'll talk about it again in a year's time. If not earlier.

HEDDA (*curtly*). I've no leanings in that direction, Judge. I don't want any – responsibilities.

BRACK. But surely you must feel some inclination to make use of that – natural talent which every woman –

HEDDA (*over by the french windows*). Oh, be quiet, I say! I often think there's only one thing for which I have any natural talent.

BRACK (*goes closer*). And what is that, if I may be so bold as to ask?

HEDDA (*stands looking out*). For boring myself to death. Now you know. (*Turns, looks towards the rear room and laughs.*) Talking of boring, here comes the professor.

BRACK (*quietly, warningly*). Now, now, now, Mrs Hedda!

> GEORGE TESMAN, *in evening dress, with gloves and hat in his hand, enters through the rear room from the right.*

TESMAN. Hedda, hasn't any message come from Eilert? What?

HEDDA. No.

TESMAN. Ah, then we'll have him here presently. You wait
and see.

BRACK. You really think he'll come?

TESMAN. Yes, I'm almost sure he will. What you were saying
about him this morning is just gossip.

BRACK. Oh?

TESMAN. Yes. Auntie Juju said she didn't believe he'd ever
dare to stand in my way again. Fancy that!

BRACK. Then everything in the garden's lovely.

TESMAN (*puts his hat, with his gloves in it, on a chair, right*). Yes,
but you really must let me wait for him as long as possible.

BRACK. We've plenty of time. No one'll be turning up at my
place before seven or half past.

TESMAN. Ah, then we can keep Hedda company a little longer.
And see if he turns up. What?

HEDDA (*picks up* BRACK'S *coat and hat and carries them over to
the corner sofa*). And if the worst comes to the worst, Mr
Loevborg can sit here and talk to me.

BRACK (*offering to take his things from her*). No, please. What
do you mean by 'if the worst comes to the worst'?

HEDDA. If he doesn't want to go with you and Tesman.

TESMAN (*looks doubtfully at her*). I say, Hedda, do you think
it'll be all right for him to stay here with you? What?
Remember Auntie Juju isn't coming.

HEDDA. Yes, but Mrs Elvsted is. The three of us can have a
cup of tea together.

TESMAN. Ah, that'll be all right.

BRACK (*smiles*). It's probably the safest solution as far as he's
concerned.

HEDDA. Why?

BRACK. My dear Mrs Tesman, you always say of my little
bachelor parties that they should only be attended by men
of the strongest principles.

HEDDA. But Mr Loevborg is a man of principle now. You
know what they say about a reformed sinner –

BERTHA *enters from the hall.*

BERTHA. Madam, there's a gentleman here who wants to see you –

HEDDA. Ask him to come in.

TESMAN (*quietly*). I'm sure it's him. By Jove. Fancy that!

EILERT LOEVBORG *enters from the hall. He is slim and lean, of the same age as* TESMAN, *but looks older and somewhat haggard. His hair and beard are of a blackish-brown; his face is long and pale, but with a couple of reddish patches on his cheekbones. He is dressed in an elegant and fairly new black suit, and carries black gloves and a top-hat in his hand. He stops just inside the door and bows abruptly. He seems somewhat embarrassed.*

(*Goes over and shakes his hand.*) My dear Eilert! How grand to see you again after all these years!

EILERT LOEVBORG (*speaks softly*). It was good of you to write, George. (*Goes nearer to* HEDDA.) May I shake hands with you, too, Mrs Tesman?

HEDDA (*accepts his hand*). Delighted to see you, Mr Loevborg. (*With a gesture.*) I don't know if you two gentlemen –

LOEVBORG (*bows slightly*). Judge Brack, I believe.

BRACK (*also with a slight bow*). Correct. We – met some years ago –

TESMAN (*puts his hands on* LOEVBORG'S *shoulders*). Now, you're to treat this house just as though it were your own home, Eilert. Isn't that right, Hedda? I hear you've decided to settle here again. What?

LOEVBORG. Yes, I have.

TESMAN. Quite understandable. Oh, by the by – I've just bought your new book. Though to tell the truth I haven't found time to read it yet.

LOEVBORG. You needn't bother.

TESMAN. Oh? Why?

LOEVBORG. There's nothing much in it.

TESMAN. By Jove, fancy hearing that from you!

BRACK. But everyone's praising it.

LOEVBORG. That was exactly what I wanted to happen. So I only wrote what I knew everyone would agree with.

BRACK. Very sensible.

TESMAN. Yes, but my dear Eilert –

LOEVBORG. I want to try to re-establish myself. To begin again – from the beginning.

TESMAN (*a little embarrassed*). Yes, I – er – suppose you do. What?

LOEVBORG (*smiles, puts down his hat and takes a package wrapped in paper from his coat pocket*). But when this gets published – George Tesman – read it. This is my real book. The one in which I have spoken with my own voice.

TESMAN. Oh, really? What's it about?

LOEVBORG. It's the sequel.

TESMAN. Sequel? To what?

LOEVBORG. To the other book.

TESMAN. The one that's just come out?

LOEVBORG. Yes.

TESMAN. But my dear Eilert, that covers the subject right up to the present day.

LOEVBORG. It does. But this is about the future.

TESMAN. The future! But, I say, we don't know anything about that.

LOEVBORG. No. But there are one or two things that need to be said about it. (*Opens the package.*) Here, have a look.

TESMAN. Surely that's not your handwriting?

LOEVBORG. I dictated it. (*Turns the pages.*) It's in two parts. The first deals with the forces that will shape our civilization. (*Turns further on towards the end.*) And the second indicates the direction in which that civilization may develop.

TESMAN. Amazing! I'd never think of writing about anything like that.

HEDDA (*by the french windows, drumming on the pane*). No. You wouldn't.

LOEVBORG (*puts the pages back into their cover and lays the package on the table*). I brought it because I thought I might possibly read you a few pages this evening.

TESMAN. I say, what a kind idea! Oh, but this evening – ? (*Glances at* BRACK) I'm not quite sure whether –

LOEVBORG. Well, some other time, then. There's no hurry.

BRACK. The truth is, Mr Loevborg, I'm giving a little dinner this evening. In Tesman's honour, you know.

LOEVBORG (*looks round for his hat*). Oh – then I mustn't –

BRACK. No, wait a minute. Won't you do me the honour of joining us?

LOEVBORG (*curtly, with decision*). No, I can't. Thank you so much.

BRACK. Oh, nonsense. Do – please. There'll only be a few of us. And I can promise you we shall have some good sport, as Hed – as Mrs Tesman puts it.

LOEVBORG. I've no doubt. Nevertheless

BRACK. You could bring your manuscript along and read it to Tesman at my place. I could lend you a room.

TESMAN. Well, yes, that's an idea. What?

HEDDA (*interposes*). But, Tesman, Mr Loevborg doesn't want to go. I'm sure Mr Loevborg would much rather sit here and have supper with me.

LOEVBORG (*looks at her*). With you, Mrs Tesman?

HEDDA. And Mrs Elvsted.

LOEVBORG. Oh. (*Casually.*) I ran into her this afternoon.

HEDDA. Did you? Well, she's coming here this evening. So you really must stay, Mr Loevborg. Otherwise she'll have no one to see her home.

LOEVBORG. That's true. Well – thank you, Mrs Tesman, I'll stay then.

HEDDA. I'll just tell the servant.

She goes to the door which leads into the hall, and rings.
BERTHA *enters.* HEDDA *talks softly to her and points towards
the rear room.* BERTHA *nods and goes out.*

TESMAN (*to* LOEVBORG, *as* HEDDA *does this*). I say, Eilert.
This new subject of yours – the – er – future – is that the one
you're going to lecture about?

LOEVBORG. Yes.

TESMAN. They told me down at the bookshop that you're
going to hold a series of lectures here during the autumn.

LOEVBORG. Yes, I am. I – hope you don't mind, Tesman.

TESMAN. Good heavens, no! But – ?

LOEVBORG. I can quite understand it might queer your pitch
a little.

TESMAN (*dejectedly*). Oh well, I can't expect you to put them
off for my sake.

LOEVBORG. I'll wait till your appointment's been announced.

TESMAN. You'll wait! But – but – aren't you going to compete
with me for the post? What?

LOEVBORG. No. I only want to defeat you in the eyes of the
world.

TESMAN. Good heavens! Then Auntie Juju was right after all!
Oh, I knew it, I knew it! Hear that, Hedda? Fancy! Eilert
doesn't want to stand in our way.

HEDDA (*curtly*): Our? Leave me out of it, please.

She goes towards the rear room, where BERTHA *is setting a
tray with decanters and glasses on the table.* HEDDA *nods
approval, and comes back into the drawing-room.* BERTHA
goes out.

TESMAN (*while this is happening*). Judge Brack, what do you
think about all this? What?

BRACK. Oh, I think honour and victory can be very splendid
things –

TESMAN. Of course they can. Still –

HEDDA (*looks at* TESMAN, *with a cold smile*). You look as if you'd been hit by a thunderbolt.

TESMAN. Yes, I feel rather like it.

BRACK. There was a black cloud looming up, Mrs Tesman. But it seems to have passed over.

HEDDA (*points towards the rear room*). Well, gentlemen, won't you go in and take a glass of cold punch?

BRACK (*glances at his watch*). One for the road? Yes, why not?

TESMAN. An admirable suggestion, Hedda. Admirable! Oh, I feel so relieved!

HEDDA. Won't you have one, too, Mr Loevborg?

LOEVBORG. No, thank you. I'd rather not.

BRACK. Great heavens, man, cold punch isn't poison. Take my word for it.

LOEVBORG. Not for everyone, perhaps.

HEDDA. I'll keep Mr Loevborg company while you drink.

TESMAN. Yes, Hedda dear, would you?

> *He and* BRACK *go into the rear room, sit down, drink punch, smoke cigarettes and talk cheerfully during the following scene.* EILERT LOEVBORG *remains standing by the stove.* HEDDA *goes to the writing-table.*

HEDDA (*raising her voice slightly*). I've some photographs I'd like to show you, if you'd care to see them. Tesman and I visited the Tyrol on our way home.

> *She comes back with an album, places it on the table by the sofa and sits in the upstage corner of the sofa.* EILERT LOEVBORG *comes towards her, stops, and looks at her. Then he takes a chair and sits down on her left, with his back towards the rear room.*

(*Opens the album.*) You see these mountains, Mr Loevborg? That's the Ortler group. Tesman has written the name underneath. You see: 'The Ortler Group near Meran.'

LOEVBORG (*has not taken his eyes from her; says softly, slowly*).
Hedda – Gabler!

HEDDA (*gives him a quick glance*). Ssh!

LOEVBORG (*repeats softly*). Hedda Gabler!

HEDDA (*looks at the album*). Yes, that used to be my name.
When we first knew each other.

LOEVBORG. And from now on – for the rest of my life – I must
teach myself never to say: Hedda Gabler.

HEDDA (*still turning the pages*). Yes, you must. You'd better
start getting into practice. The sooner the better.

LOEVBORG (*bitterly*). Hedda Gabler married? And to George
Tesman!

HEDDA. Yes. Well – that's life.

LOEVBORG. Oh, Hedda, Hedda! How could you throw yourself away like that?

HEDDA (*looks sharply at him*). Stop it.

LOEVBORG. What do you mean?

TESMAN *comes in and goes towards the sofa.*

HEDDA (*hears him coming and says casually*). And this, Mr
Loevborg, is the view from the Ampezzo valley. Look at
those mountains. (*Glances affectionately up at* TESMAN.)
What did you say those curious mountains were called, dear?

TESMAN. Let me have a look. Oh, those are the Dolomites.

HEDDA. Of course. Those are the Dolomites, Mr Loevborg.

TESMAN. Hedda, I just wanted to ask you, can't we bring
some punch in here? A glass for you, anyway. What?

HEDDA. Thank you, yes. And a biscuit or two, perhaps.

TESMAN. You wouldn't like a cigarette?

HEDDA. No.

TESMAN. Right.

He goes into the rear room and over to the right. BRACK *is
seated there, glancing occasionally at* HEDDA *and* LOEV-
BORG.

LOEVBORG (*softly, as before*). Answer me, Hedda. How could you do it?

HEDDA (*apparently absorbed in the album*). If you go on calling me Hedda I won't talk to you any more.

LOEVBORG. Mayn't I even when we're alone?

HEDDA. No. You can think it. But you mustn't say it.

LOEVBORG. Oh, I see. Because you love George Tesman.

HEDDA (*glances at him and smiles*). Love? Don't be funny.

LOEVBORG. You don't love him?

HEDDA. I don't intend to be unfaithful to him. That's not what I want.

LOEVBORG. Hedda – just tell me one thing –

HEDDA. Ssh!

TESMAN *enters from the rear room, carrying a tray.*

TESMAN. Here we are! Here come the refreshments.

He puts the tray down on the table.

HEDDA. Why didn't you ask the servant to bring it in?

TESMAN (*fills the glasses*). I like waiting on you, Hedda.

HEDDA. But you've filled both glasses. Mr Loevborg doesn't want to drink.

TESMAN. Yes, but Mrs Elvsted'll be here soon.

HEDDA. Oh yes, that's true. Mrs Elvsted –

TESMAN. Had you forgotten her? What?

HEDDA. We're so absorbed with these photographs. (*Shows him one.*) You remember this little village?

TESMAN. Oh, that one down by the Brenner Pass. We spent a night there –

HEDDA. Yes, and met all those amusing people.

TESMAN. Oh yes, it was there, wasn't it? By Jove, if only we could have had you with us, Eilert! Ah, well.

He goes back into the other room and sits down with BRACK.

LOEVBORG. Tell me one thing, Hedda.

HEDDA. Yes?

LOEVBORG. Didn't you love me either? Not – just a little?

HEDDA. Well now, I wonder? No, I think we were just good friends. (*Smiles.*) You certainly poured your heart out to me.

LOEVBORG. You begged me to.

HEDDA. Looking back on it, there was something beautiful and fascinating – and brave – about the way we told each other everything. That secret friendship no one else knew about.

LOEVBORG. Yes, Hedda, yes! Do you remember? How I used to come up to your father's house in the afternoon – and the General sat by the window and read his newspapers – with his back towards us –

HEDDA. And we sat on the sofa in the corner –

LOEVBORG. Always reading the same illustrated magazine –

HEDDA. We hadn't any photograph album.

LOEVBORG. Yes, Hedda. I regarded you as a kind of confessor. Told you things about myself which no one else knew about – then. Those days and nights of drinking and – oh, Hedda, what power did you have to make me confess such things?

HEDDA. Power? You think I had some power over you?

LOEVBORG. Yes – I don't know how else to explain it. And all those – oblique questions you asked me –

HEDDA. You knew what they meant.

LOEVBORG. But that you could sit there and ask me such questions! So unashamedly –

HEDDA. I thought you said they were oblique.

LOEVBORG. Yes, but you asked them so unashamedly. That you could question me about – about that kind of thing!

HEDDA. You answered willingly enough.

LOEVBORG. Yes – that's what I can't understand – looking back on it. But tell me, Hedda – what you felt for me – wasn't that – love? When you asked me those questions and made me confess my sins to you, wasn't it because you wanted to wash me clean?

HEDDA. No, not exactly.

LOEVBORG. Why did you do it, then?

HEDDA. Do you find it so incredible that a young girl, given the chance in secret, should want to be allowed a glimpse into a forbidden world of whose existence she is supposed to be ignorant?

LOEVBORG. So that was it?

HEDDA. One reason. One reason – I think.

LOEVBORG. You didn't love me, then. You just wanted – knowledge. But if that was so, why did you break it off?

HEDDA. That was your fault.

LOEVBORG. It was you who put an end to it.

HEDDA. Yes, when I realized that our friendship was threatening to develop into something – something else. Shame on you, Eilert Loevborg! How could you abuse the trust of your dearest friend?

LOEVBORG (*clenches his fist*). Oh, why didn't you do it? Why didn't you shoot me dead? As you threatened to!

HEDDA. I was afraid. Of the scandal.

LOEVBORG. Yes, Hedda. You're a coward at heart.

HEDDA. A dreadful coward. (*Changes her tone.*) Luckily for you. Well, now you've found consolation with the Elvsteds.

LOEVBORG. I know what Thea's been telling you.

HEDDA. I dare say you told her about us.

LOEVBORG. Not a word. She's too silly to understand that kind of thing.

HEDDA. Silly?

LOEVBORG. She's silly about that kind of thing.

HEDDA. And I'm a coward. (*Leans closer to him, without looking him in the eyes, and says quietly.*) But let me tell you something. Something you don't know.

LOEVBORG (*tensely*). Yes?

HEDDA. My failure to shoot you wasn't my worst act of cowardice that evening.

LOEVBORG (*looks at her for a moment, realizes her meaning, and*

whispers passionately). Oh, Hedda! Hedda Gabler! Now I
see what was behind those questions. Yes! It wasn't knowledge you wanted! It was life!

HEDDA (*flashes a look at him and says quietly*). Take care!
Don't you delude yourself!

> *It has begun to grow dark.* BERTHA, *from outside, opens the
> door leading into the hall.*

(HEDDA *closes the album with a snap and cries, smiling.*) Ah, at
last! Come in, Thea dear!

> MRS ELVSTED *enters from the hall, in evening dress. The
> door is closed behind her.*

(HEDDA *on the sofa, stretches out her arms towards her.*) Thea
darling, I thought you were never coming!

> MRS ELVSTED *makes a slight bow to the gentlemen in the rear
> room as she passes the open doorway, and they to her. Then
> she goes to the table and holds out her hand to* HEDDA.
> EILERT LOEVBORG *has risen from his chair. He and* MRS
> ELVSTED *nod silently to each other.*

MRS ELVSTED. Perhaps I ought to go in and say a few words to
your husband?

HEDDA. Oh, there's no need. They're happy by themselves.
They'll be going soon.

MRS ELVSTED. Going?

HEDDA. Yes, they're off on a spree this evening.

MRS ELVSTED (*quickly, to* LOEVBORG). You're not going with
them?

LOEVBORG. No.

HEDDA. Mr Loevborg is staying here with us.

MRS ELVSTED (*takes a chair and is about to sit down beside him*).
Oh, how nice it is to be here!

HEDDA. No, Thea darling, not there. Come over here and sit
beside me. I want to be in the middle.

MRS ELVSTED. Yes, just as you wish.

> *She goes round the table and sits on the sofa, on* HEDDA'S *right.* LOEVBORG *sits down again in his chair.*

LOEVBORG (*after a short pause, to* HEDDA). Isn't she lovely to look at?

HEDDA (*strokes her hair gently*). Only to look at?

LOEVBORG. Yes. We're just good friends. We trust each other implicitly. We can talk to each other quite unashamedly.

HEDDA. No need to be oblique?

MRS ELVSTED (*nestles close to* HEDDA *and says quietly*). Oh, Hedda, I'm so happy. Imagine – he says I've inspired him!

HEDDA (*looks at her with a smile*). Dear Thea! Does he really?

LOEVBORG. She has the courage of her convictions, Mrs Tesman.

MRS ELVSTED. I? Courage?

LOEVBORG. Absolute courage. Where friendship is concerned.

HEDDA. Yes. Courage. Yes. If only one had that –

LOEVBORG. Yes?

HEDDA. One might be able to live. In spite of everything. (*Changes her tone suddenly.*) Well, Thea darling, now you're going to drink a nice glass of cold punch.

MRS ELVSTED. No thank you. I never drink anything like that.

HEDDA. Oh. You, Mr Loevborg?

LOEVBORG. Thank you, I don't either.

MRS ELVSTED. No, he doesn't, either.

HEDDA (*looks into his eyes*). But if I want you to.

LOEVBORG. That doesn't make any difference.

HEDDA (*laughs*). Have I no power over you at all? Poor me!

LOEVBORG. Not where this is concerned.

HEDDA. Seriously, I think you should. For your own sake.

MRS ELVSTED. Hedda!

LOEVBORG. Why?

HEDDA. Or perhaps I should say for other people's sake.

LOEVBORG. What do you mean?

HEDDA. People might think you didn't feel absolutely and unashamedly sure of yourself. In your heart of hearts.

MRS ELVSTED (*quietly*). Oh, Hedda, no!

LOEVBORG. People can think what they like. For the present.

MRS ELVSTED (*happily*). Yes, that's true.

HEDDA. I saw it so clearly in Judge Brack a few minutes ago.

LOEVBORG. Oh. What did you see?

HEDDA. He smiled so scornfully when he saw you were afraid to go in there and drink with them.

LOEVBORG. Afraid! I wanted to stay here and talk to you.

MRS ELVSTED. That was only natural, Hedda.

HEDDA. But the Judge wasn't to know that. I saw him wink at Tesman when you showed you didn't dare to join their wretched little party.

LOEVBORG. Didn't dare! Are you saying I didn't dare?

HEDDA. I'm not saying so. But that was what Judge Brack thought.

LOEVBORG. Well, let him.

HEDDA. You're not going, then?

LOEVBORG. I'm staying here with you and Thea.

MRS ELVSTED. Yes, Hedda, of course he is.

HEDDA (*smiles, and nods approvingly to* LOEVBORG). Firm as a rock! A man of principle! That's how a man should be! (*Turns to* MRS ELVSTED *and strokes her cheek.*) Didn't I tell you so this morning when you came here in such a panic – ?

LOEVBORG (*starts*). Panic?

MRS ELVSTED (*frightened*). Hedda! But – Hedda!

HEDDA. Well, now you can see for yourself. There's no earthly need for you to get scared to death just because – (*Stops.*) Well! Let's all three cheer up and enjoy ourselves.

LOEVBORG. Mrs Tesman, would you mind explaining to me what this is all about?

MRS ELVSTED. Oh, my God, my God, Hedda, what are you saying? What are you doing?

HEDDA. Keep calm. That horrid Judge has his eye on you.

LOEVBORG. Scared to death, were you? For my sake?

MRS ELVSTED (*quietly, trembling*). Oh, Hedda! You've made me so unhappy!

LOEVBORG (*looks coldly at her for a moment. His face is distorted*). So that was how much you trusted me.

MRS ELVSTED. Eilert dear, please listen to me –

LOEVBORG (*takes one of the glasses of punch, raises it and says quietly, hoarsely*). Skoal, Thea!

He empties the glass, puts it down and picks up one of the others.

MRS ELVSTED (*quietly*). Hedda, Hedda! Why did you want this to happen?

HEDDA. *I* – want it? Are you mad?

LOEVBORG. Skoal to you, too, Mrs Tesman. Thanks for telling me the truth. Here's to the truth!

He empties his glass and refills it.

HEDDA (*puts her hand on his arm*). Steady. That's enough for now. Don't forget the party.

MRS ELVSTED. No, no, no!

HEDDA. Ssh! They're looking at you.

LOEVBORG (*puts down his glass*). Thea, tell me the truth –

MRS ELVSTED. Yes!

LOEVBORG. Did your husband know you were following me?

MRS ELVSTED. Oh, Hedda!

LOEVBORG. Did you and he have an agreement that you should come here and keep an eye on me? Perhaps he gave you the idea? After all, he's a magistrate. I suppose he needed me back in his office. Or did he miss my companionship at the card-table?

MRS ELVSTED (*quietly, sobbing*). Eilert, Eilert!

LOEVBORG (*seizes a glass and is about to fill it*). Let's drink to him, too.

HEDDA. No more now. Remember you're going to read your book to Tesman.

LOEVBORG (*calm again, puts down his glass*). That was silly of me, Thea. To take it like that, I mean. Don't be angry with me, my dear. You'll see – yes, and they'll see, too – that though I fell, I – I have raised myself up again. With your help, Thea.

MRS ELVSTED (*happily*). Oh, thank God!

> BRACK *has meanwhile glanced at his watch. He and* TESMAN *get up and come into the drawing-room.*

BRACK (*takes his hat and overcoat*). Well, Mrs Tesman, it's time for us to go.

HEDDA. Yes, I suppose it must be.

LOEVBORG (*gets up*). Time for me, too, Judge.

MRS ELVSTED (*quietly, pleadingly*). Eilert, please don't!

HEDDA (*pinches her arm*). They can hear you.

MRS ELVSTED (*gives a little cry*). Oh!

LOEVBORG (*to* BRACK). You were kind enough to ask me to join you.

BRACK. Are you coming?

LOEVBORG. If I may.

BRACK. Delighted.

LOEVBORG (*puts the paper package in his pocket and says to* TESMAN). I'd like to show you one or two things before I send it off to the printer.

TESMAN. I say, that'll be fun. Fancy – ! Oh, but, Hedda, how'll Mrs Elvsted get home? What?

HEDDA. Oh, we'll manage somehow.

LOEVBORG (*glances over towards the ladies*). Mrs Elvsted? I shall come back and collect her, naturally. (*Goes closer.*) About ten o'clock, Mrs Tesman? Will that suit you?

HEDDA. Yes. That'll suit me admirably.

TESMAN. Good, that's settled. But you mustn't expect me back so early, Hedda.

HEDDA. Stay as long as you c – as long as ₎ou like, dear.

MRS ELVSTED (*trying to hide her anxiety*). Well then, Mr Loevborg, I'll wait here till you come.

LOEVBORG (*his hat in his hand*). Pray do, Mrs Elvsted.

BRACK. Well, gentlemen, now the party begins. I trust that,
in the words of a certain fair lady, we shall enjoy good sport.

HEDDA. What a pity the fair lady can't be there, invisible.

BRACK. Why invisible?

HEDDA. So as to be able to hear some of your uncensored
witticisms, your honour.

BRACK (*laughs*). Oh, I shouldn't advise the fair lady to do that.

TESMAN (*laughs, too*). I say, Hedda, that's good. What!

BRACK. Well, good night, ladies, good night!

LOEVBORG (*bows farewell*). About ten o'clock then.

> BRACK, LOEVBORG *and* TESMAN *go out through the hall.
> As they do so,* BERTHA *enters from the rear room with a
> lighted lamp. She puts it on the drawing-room table, then
> goes out the way she came.*

MRS ELVSTED (*has got up and is walking uneasily to and fro*).
Oh, Hedda, Hedda! How is all this going to end?

HEDDA. At ten o'clock, then. He'll be here. I can see him.
With a crown of vine leaves in his hair. Burning and unashamed!

MRS ELVSTED. Oh, I do hope so!

HEDDA. Can't you see? Then he'll be himself again! He'll be
a free man for the rest of his days!

MRS ELVSTED. Please God you're right.

HEDDA. That's how he'll come! (*Gets up and goes closer.*) You
can doubt him as much as you like. I believe in him! Now
we'll see which of us –

MRS ELVSTED. You're after something, Hedda.

HEDDA. Yes, I am. For once in my life I want to have the
power to shape a man's destiny.

MRS ELVSTED. Haven't you that power already?

HEDDA. No, I haven't. I've never had it.

MRS ELVSTED. What about your husband?

HEDDA. Him! Oh, if you could only understand how poor I am. And you're allowed to be so rich, so rich! (*Clasps her passionately.*) I think I'll burn your hair off after all!

MRS ELVSTED. Let me go! Let me go! You frighten me, Hedda!

BERTHA (*in the open doorway*). I've laid tea in the dining-room, madam.

HEDDA. Good, we're coming.

MRS ELVSTED. No, no, no! I'd rather go home alone! Now – at once!

HEDDA. Rubbish! First you're going to have some tea, you little idiot. And then – at ten o'clock – Eilert Loevborg will come. With a crown of vine leaves in his hair!

She drags MRS ELVSTED *almost forcibly towards the open doorway.*

Act Three

The same. The curtains are drawn across the open doorway, and also across the french windows. The lamp, half turned down, with a shade over it, is burning on the table. In the stove, the door of which is open, a fire has been burning, but it is now almost out. MRS ELVSTED, *wrapped in a large shawl and with her feet resting on a footstool, is sitting near the stove, huddled in the armchair.* HEDDA *is lying asleep on the sofa, fully dressed, with a blanket over her.*

MRS ELVSTED (*after a pause, suddenly sits up in her chair and listens tensely. Then she sinks wearily back again and sighs.*)
Not back yet! Oh, God! Oh, God! Not back yet!

> BERTHA *tiptoes cautiously in from the hall. She has a letter in her hand.*

(*Turns and whispers.*) What is it? Has someone come?
BERTHA (*quietly*). Yes, a servant's just called with this letter.
MRS ELVSTED (*quickly, holding out her hand*). A letter! Give it to me!
BERTHA. But it's for the Doctor, madam.
MRS ELVSTED. Oh, I see.
BERTHA. Miss Tesman's maid brought it. I'll leave it here on the table.
MRS ELVSTED. Yes, do.
BERTHA (*puts down the letter*). I'd better put the lamp out. It's starting to smoke.
MRS ELVSTED. Yes, put it out. It'll soon be daylight.
BERTHA (*puts out the lamp*). It's daylight already, madam.
MRS ELVSTED. Yes. Broad day. And not home yet.
BERTHA. Oh dear, I was afraid this would happen.
MRS ELVSTED. Were you?

BERTHA. Yes. When I heard that a certain gentleman had returned to town, and saw him go off with them. I've heard all about him.

MRS ELVSTED. Don't talk so loud. You'll wake your mistress.

BERTHA (*looks at the sofa and sighs*). Yes. Let her go on sleeping, poor dear. Shall I put some more wood on the fire?

MRS ELVSTED. Thank you, don't bother on my account.

BERTHA. Very good.

She goes quietly out through the hall.

HEDDA (*wakes as the door closes and looks up*). What's that?

MRS ELVSTED. It was only the maid.

HEDDA (*looks round*). What am I doing here? Oh, now I remember. (*Sits up on the sofa, stretches herself and rubs her eyes.*) What time is it, Thea?

MRS ELVSTED. It's gone seven.

HEDDA. When did Tesman get back?

MRS ELVSTED. He's not back yet.

HEDDA. Not home yet?

MRS ELVSTED (*gets up*). No one's come.

HEDDA. And we sat up waiting for them till four o'clock.

MRS ELVSTED. God! How I waited for him!

HEDDA (*yawns and says with her hand in front of her mouth*). Oh, dear. We might have saved ourselves the trouble.

MRS ELVSTED. Did you manage to sleep?

HEDDA. Oh, yes. Quite well, I think. Didn't you get any?

MRS ELVSTED. Not a wink. I couldn't, Hedda. I just couldn't.

HEDDA (*gets up and comes over to her*). Now, now, now. There's nothing to worry about. I know what's happened.

MRS ELVSTED. What? Please tell me.

HEDDA. Well, obviously the party went on very late –

MRS ELVSTED. Oh dear, I suppose it must have. But –

HEDDA. And Tesman didn't want to come home and wake us all up in the middle of the night. (*Laughs.*) Probably wasn't too keen to show his face either, after a spree like that.

MRS ELVSTED. But where could he have gone?

HEDDA. I should think he's probably slept at his aunts'. They keep his old room for him.

MRS ELVSTED. No, he can't be with them. A letter came for him just now from Miss Tesman. It's over there.

HEDDA. Oh? (*Looks at the envelope.*) Yes, it's Auntie Juju's handwriting. Well, he must still be at Judge Brack's, then. And Eilert Loevborg is sitting there, reading to him. With a crown of vine leaves in his hair.

MRS ELVSTED. Hedda, you're only saying that. You don't believe it.

HEDDA. Thea, you really are a little fool.

MRS ELVSTED. Perhaps I am.

HEDDA. You look tired to death.

MRS ELVSTED. Yes. I am tired to death.

HEDDA. Go to my room and lie down for a little. Do as I say, now; don't argue.

MRS ELVSTED. No, no. I couldn't possibly sleep.

HEDDA. Of course you can.

MRS ELVSTED. But your husband'll be home soon. And I must know at once –

HEDDA. I'll tell you when he comes.

MRS ELVSTED. Promise me, Hedda?

HEDDA. Yes, don't worry. Go and get some sleep.

MRS ELVSTED. Thank you. All right, I'll try.

> *She goes out through the rear room.* HEDDA *goes to the french windows and draws the curtains. Broad daylight floods into the room. She goes to the writing-table, takes a small hand-mirror from it and arranges her hair. Then she goes to the door leading into the hall and presses the bell. After a few moments,* BERTHA *enters.*

BERTHA. Did you want anything, madam?

HEDDA. Yes, put some more wood on the fire. I'm freezing.

BERTHA. Bless you, I'll soon have this room warmed up. (*She*

*rakes the embers together and puts a fresh piece of wood on
them. Suddenly she stops and listens.*) There's someone at the
front door, madam.

HEDDA. Well, go and open it. I'll see to the fire.

BERTHA. It'll burn up in a moment.

> *She goes out through the hall.* HEDDA *kneels on the footstool
> and puts more wood in the stove. After a few seconds,*
> GEORGE TESMAN *enters from the hall. He looks tired, and
> rather worried. He tiptoes towards the open doorway and is
> about to slip through the curtains.*

HEDDA (*at the stove, without looking up*). Good morning.

TESMAN (*turns*). Hedda! (*Comes nearer.*) Good heavens, are
you up already? What?

HEDDA. Yes I got up very early this morning.

TESMAN. I was sure you'd still be sleeping. Fancy that!

HEDDA. Don't talk so loud. Mrs Elvsted's asleep in my room.

TESMAN. Mrs Elvsted? Has she stayed the night here?

HEDDA. Yes. No one came to escort her home.

TESMAN. Oh. No, I suppose not.

HEDDA (*closes the door of the stove and gets up*). Well. Was it
fun?

TESMAN. Have you been anxious about me? What?

HEDDA. Not in the least. I asked if you'd had fun.

TESMAN. Oh yes, rather! Well, I thought, for once in a while –!
The first part was the best; when Eilert read his book to me.
We arrived over an hour too early – what about that, eh?
Fancy – ! Brack had a lot of things to see to, so Eilert read
to me.

HEDDA (*sits at the right-hand side of the table*). Well? Tell me
about it.

TESMAN (*sits on a footstool by the stove*). Honestly, Hedda,
you've no idea what a book that's going to be. It's really one
of the most remarkable things that's ever been written. By
Jove!

HEDDA. Oh, never mind about the book –

TESMAN. I'm going to make a confession to you, Hedda. When he'd finished reading a sort of beastly feeling came over me.

HEDDA. Beastly feeling?

TESMAN. I found myself envying Eilert for being able to write like that. Imagine that, Hedda!

HEDDA. Yes. I can imagine.

TESMAN. What a tragedy that with all those gifts he should be so incorrigible.

HEDDA. You mean he's less afraid of life than most men?

TESMAN. Good heavens, no. He just doesn't know the meaning of the word moderation.

HEDDA. What happened afterwards?

TESMAN. Well, looking back on it, I suppose you might almost call it an orgy, Hedda.

HEDDA. Had he vine leaves in his hair?

TESMAN. Vine leaves? No, I didn't see any of them. He made a long, rambling oration in honour of the woman who'd inspired him to write this book. Yes, those were the words he used.

HEDDA. Did he name her?

TESMAN. No. But I suppose it must be Mrs Elvsted. You wait and see!

HEDDA. Where did you leave him?

TESMAN. On the way home. We left in a bunch – the last of us, that is – and Brack came with us to get a little fresh air. Well, then, you see, we agreed we ought to see Eilert home. He'd had a drop too much.

HEDDA. You don't say?

TESMAN. But now comes the funny part, Hedda. Or I should really say the tragic part. Oh, I'm almost ashamed to tell you. For Eilert's sake, I mean –

HEDDA. Why, what happened?

TESMAN. Well, you see, as we were walking towards town I

happened to drop behind for a minute. Only for a minute – er – you understand –

HEDDA. Yes, yes – ?

TESMAN. Well then, when I ran on to catch them up, what do you think I found by the roadside. What?

HEDDA. How on earth should I know?

TESMAN. You mustn't tell anyone, Hedda. What? Promise me that – for Eilert's sake. (*Takes a package wrapped in paper from his coat pocket.*) Just fancy! I found this.

HEDDA. Isn't this the one he brought here yesterday?

TESMAN. Yes! The whole of that precious, irreplaceable manuscript! And he went and lost it! Didn't even notice! What about that? Tragic.

HEDDA. But why didn't you give it back to him?

TESMAN. I didn't dare to, in the state he was in.

HEDDA. Didn't you tell any of the others?

TESMAN. Good heavens, no. I didn't want to do that. For Eilert's sake, you understand.

HEDDA. Then no one else knows you have his manuscript?

TESMAN. No. And no one must be allowed to know.

HEDDA. Didn't it come up in the conversation later?

TESMAN. I didn't get a chance to talk to him any more. As soon as we got into the outskirts of town, he and one or two of the others gave us the slip. Disappeared, by Jove!

HEDDA. Oh? I suppose they took him home.

TESMAN. Yes, I imagine that was the idea. Brack left us, too.

HEDDA. And what have you been up to since then?

TESMAN. Well, I and one or two of the others – awfully jolly chaps, they were – went back to where one of them lived and had a cup of morning coffee. Morning-after coffee – what? Ah, well. I'll just lie down for a bit and give Eilert time to sleep it off, poor chap, then I'll run over and give this back to him.

HEDDA (*holds out her hand for the package*). No, don't do that. Not just yet. Let me read it first.

TESMAN. Oh no, really, Hedda dear, honestly, I daren't do that.

HEDDA. Daren't?

TESMAN. No – imagine how desperate he'll be when he wakes up and finds his manuscript's missing. He hasn't any copy, you see. He told me so himself.

HEDDA. Can't a thing like that be rewritten?

TESMAN. Oh no, not possibly, I shouldn't think. I mean, the inspiration, you know –

HEDDA. Oh, yes, I'd forgotten that. (*Casually.*) By the way, there's a letter for you.

TESMAN. Is there? Fancy that!

HEDDA (*holds it out to him*). It came early this morning.

TESMAN. I say, it's from Auntie Juju! What on earth can it be? (*Puts the package on the other footstool, opens the letter, reads it and jumps up.*) Oh, Hedda! She says poor Auntie Rena's dying.

HEDDA. Well, we've been expecting that.

TESMAN. She says if I want to see her I must go quickly. I'll run over at once.

HEDDA (*hides a smile*). Run?

TESMAN. Hedda dear, I suppose you wouldn't like to come with me? What about that, eh?

HEDDA (*gets up and says wearily and with repulsion*). No, no, don't ask me to do anything like that. I can't bear illness or death. I loathe anything ugly.

TESMAN. Yes, yes. Of course. (*In a dither.*) My hat? My overcoat? Oh yes, in the hall. I do hope I won't get there too late, Hedda! What?

HEDDA. You'll be all right if you run.

BERTHA *enters from the hall.*

BERTHA. Judge Brack's outside and wants to know if he can come in.

TESMAN. At this hour? No, I can't possibly receive him now.

HEDDA. I can. (*To* BERTHA.) Ask his honour to come in.

BERTHA *goes.*

(*Whispers quickly.*) The manuscript, Tesman.

She snatches it from the footstool.

TESMAN. Yes, give it to me.

HEDDA. No, I'll look after it for now.

She goes over to the writing-table and puts it in the bookcase. TESMAN *stands dithering, unable to get his gloves on.* JUDGE BRACK *enters from the hall.*

(*Nods to him.*) Well, you're an early bird.

BRACK. Yes, aren't I? (*To* TESMAN.) Are you up and about, too?

TESMAN. Yes, I've got to go and see my aunts. Poor Auntie Rena's dying.

BRACK. Oh dear, is she? Then you mustn't let me detain you. At so tragic a –

TESMAN. Yes, I really must run. Good-bye! Good-bye!

He runs out through the hall.

HEDDA (*goes nearer*). You seem to have had excellent sport last night – Judge.

BRACK. Indeed yes, Mrs Hedda. I haven't even had time to take my clothes off.

HEDDA. *You* haven't either?

BRACK. As you see. What's Tesman told you about last night's escapades?

HEDDA. Oh, only some boring story about having gone and drunk coffee somewhere.

BRACK. Yes, I've heard about that coffee-party. Eilert Loevborg wasn't with them, I gather?

HEDDA. No, they took him home first.

BRACK. Did Tesman go with him?

HEDDA. No, one or two of the others, he said.

BRACK (*smiles*). George Tesman is a credulous man, Mrs Hedda.

HEDDA. God knows. But – has something happened?

BRACK. Well, yes, I'm afraid it has.

HEDDA. I see. Sit down and tell me.

> *She sits on the left of the table,* BRACK *at the long side of it, near her.*

Well?

BRACK. I had a special reason for keeping track of my guests last night. Or perhaps I should say some of my guests.

HEDDA. Including Eilert Loevborg?

BRACK. I must confess – yes.

HEDDA. You're beginning to make me curious.

BRACK. Do you know where he and some of my other guests spent the latter half of last night, Mrs Hedda?

HEDDA. Tell me. If it won't shock me.

BRACK. Oh, I don't think it'll shock you. They found themselves participating in an exceedingly animated *soirée*.

HEDDA. Of a sporting character?

BRACK. Of a highly sporting character.

HEDDA. Tell me more.

BRACK. Loevborg had received an invitation in advance – as had the others. I knew all about that. But he had refused. As you know, he's become a new man.

HEDDA. Up at the Elvsteds', yes. But he went?

BRACK. Well, you see, Mrs Hedda, last night at my house, unhappily, the spirit moved him.

HEDDA. Yes, I hear he became inspired.

BRACK. Somewhat violently inspired. And as a result, I suppose, his thoughts strayed. We men, alas, don't always stick to our principles as firmly as we should.

HEDDA. I'm sure you're an exception, Judge Brack. But go on about Loevborg.

BRACK. Well, to cut a long story short, he ended up in the establishment of a certain Mademoiselle Danielle.

HEDDA. Mademoiselle Danielle?

BRACK. She was holding the *soirée*. For a selected circle of friends and admirers.

HEDDA. Has she got red hair?

BRACK. She has.

HEDDA. A singer of some kind?

BRACK. Yes – among other accomplishments. She's also a celebrated huntress – of men, Mrs Hedda. I'm sure you've heard about her. Eilert Loevborg used to be one of her most ardent patrons. In his salad days.

HEDDA. And how did all this end?

BRACK. Not entirely amicably, from all accounts. Mademoiselle Danielle began by receiving him with the utmost tenderness and ended by resorting to her fists.

HEDDA. Against Loevborg?

BRACK. Yes. He accused her, or her friends, of having robbed him. He claimed his pocket-book had been stolen. Among other things. In short, he seems to have made a blood-thirsty scene.

HEDDA. And what did this lead to?

BRACK. It led to a general free-for-all, in which both sexes participated. Fortunately, in the end the police arrived.

HEDDA. The police, too?

BRACK. Yes. I'm afraid it may turn out to be rather an expensive joke for Master Eilert. Crazy fool!

HEDDA. Oh?

BRACK. Apparently he put up a very violent resistance. Hit one of the constables on the ear and tore his uniform. He had to accompany them to the police station.

HEDDA. Where did you learn all this?

BRACK. From the police.

HEDDA (*to herself*). So that's what happened. He didn't have a crown of vine leaves in his hair.

BRACK. Vine leaves, Mrs Hedda?

HEDDA (*in her normal voice again*). But, tell me, Judge, why do you take such a close interest in Eilert Loevborg?

BRACK. For one thing it'll hardly be a matter of complete indifference to me if it's revealed in court that he came there straight from my house.

HEDDA. Will it come to court?

BRACK. Of course. Well, I don't regard that as particularly serious. Still, I thought it my duty, as a friend of the family, to give you and your husband a full account of his nocturnal adventures.

HEDDA. Why?

BRACK. Because I've a shrewd suspicion that he's hoping to use you as a kind of screen.

HEDDA. What makes you think that?

BRACK. Oh, for heaven's sake, Mrs Hedda, we're not blind. You wait and see. This Mrs Elvsted won't be going back to her husband just yet.

HEDDA. Well, if there were anything between those two there are plenty of other places where they could meet.

BRACK. Not in anyone's home. From now on every respectable house will once again be closed to Eilert Loevborg.

HEDDA. And mine should be, too, you mean?

BRACK. Yes. I confess I should find it more than irksome if this gentleman were to be granted unrestricted access to this house. If he were superfluously to intrude into –

HEDDA. The triangle?

BRACK. Precisely. For me it would be like losing a home.

HEDDA (*looks at him and smiles*). I see. You want to be the cock of the walk.

BRACK (*nods slowly and lowers his voice*). Yes, that is my aim. And I shall fight for it with – every weapon at my disposal.

HEDDA (*as her smile fades*). You're a dangerous man, aren't you? When you really want something.

BRACK. You think so?

HEDDA. Yes, I'm beginning to think so. I'm deeply thankful you haven't any kind of hold over me.

BRACK (*laughs equivocally*). Well, well, Mrs Hedda – perhaps you're right. If I had, who knows what I might not think up?

HEDDA. Come, Judge Brack. That sounds almost like a threat.

BRACK (*gets up*). Heaven forbid! In the creation of a triangle – and its continuance – the question of compulsion should never arise.

HEDDA. Exactly what I was thinking.

BRACK. Well, I've said what I came to say. I must be getting back. Good-bye, Mrs Hedda. (*Goes towards the french windows.*)

HEDDA (*gets up*). Are you going out through the garden?

BRACK. Yes, it's shorter.

HEDDA. Yes. And it's the back door, isn't it?

BRACK. I've nothing against back doors. They can be quite intriguing – sometimes.

HEDDA. When people fire pistols out of them, for example?

BRACK (*in the doorway, laughs*). Oh, people don't shoot tame cocks.

HEDDA (*laughs, too*). I suppose not. When they've only got one.

> *They nod good-bye, laughing. He goes. She closes the french windows behind him, and stands for a moment, looking out pensively. Then she walks across the room and glances through the curtains in the open doorway. Goes to the writing-table, takes* LOEVBORG'S *package from the bookcase and is about to turn through the pages when* BERTHA *is heard remonstrating loudly in the hall.* HEDDA *turns and listens. She hastily puts the package back in the drawer, locks it and puts the key on the inkstand.* EILERT LOEVBORG, *with his overcoat on and his hat in his hand, throws the door open. He looks somewhat confused and excited.*

LOEVBORG (*shouts as he enters*). I must come in, I tell you! Let me pass!

He closes the door, turns, sees HEDDA, *controls himself immediately and bows.*

HEDDA (*at the writing-table*). Well, Mr Loevborg, this is rather a late hour to be collecting Thea.

LOEVBORG. And an early hour to call on you. Please forgive me.

HEDDA. How do you know she's still here?

LOEVBORG. They told me at her lodgings that she has been out all night.

HEDDA (*goes to the table*). Did you notice anything about their behaviour when they told you?

LOEVBORG (*looks at her, puzzled*). Notice anything?

HEDDA. Did they sound as if they thought it – strange?

LOEVBORG (*suddenly understands*). Oh, I see what you mean. I'm dragging her down with me. No, as a matter of fact I didn't notice anything. I suppose Tesman isn't up yet?

HEDDA. No, I don't think so.

LOEVBORG. When did he get home?

HEDDA. Very late.

LOEVBORG. Did he tell you anything?

HEDDA. Yes. I gather you had a merry party at Judge Brack's last night.

LOEVBORG. He didn't tell you anything else?

HEDDA. I don't think so. I was so terribly sleepy –

MRS ELVSTED *comes through the curtains in the open doorway.*

MRS ELVSTED (*runs towards him*). Oh, Eilert! At last!

LOEVBORG. Yes – at last. And too late.

MRS ELVSTED. What is too late?

LOEVBORG. Everything – now. I'm finished, Thea.

MRS ELVSTED. Oh, no, no! Don't say that!

LOEVBORG. You'll say it yourself, when you've heard what I –

MRS ELVSTED. I don't want to hear anything!

HEDDA. Perhaps you'd rather speak to her alone? I'd better go.

LOEVBORG. No, stay.

MRS ELVSTED. But I don't want to hear anything, I tell you!

LOEVBORG. It's not about last night.

MRS ELVSTED. Then what – ?

LOEVBORG. I want to tell you that from now on we must stop seeing each other.

MRS ELVSTED. Stop seeing each other!

HEDDA (*involuntarily*). I knew it!

LOEVBORG. I have no further use for you, Thea.

MRS ELVSTED. You can stand there and say that! No further use for me! Surely I can go on helping you? We'll go on working together, won't we?

LOEVBORG. I don't intend to do any more work from now on.

MRS ELVSTED (*desperately*). Then what use have I for my life?

LOEVBORG. You must try to live as if you had never known me.

MRS ELVSTED. But I can't!

LOEVBORG. Try to, Thea. Go back home –

MRS ELVSTED. Never! I want to be wherever you are! I won't let myself be driven away like this! I want to stay here – and be with you when the book comes out.

HEDDA (*whispers*). Ah, yes! The book!

LOEVBORG (*looks at her*). Our book; Thea's and mine. It belongs to both of us.

MRS ELVSTED. Oh, yes! I feel that, too! And I've a right to be with you when it comes into the world. I want to see people respect and honour you again. And the joy! The joy! I want to share it with you!

LOEVBORG. Thea – our book will never come into the world.

HEDDA. Ah!

MRS ELVSTED. Not – ?

LOEVBORG. It cannot. Ever.

MRS ELVSTED. Eilert – what have you done with the manuscript?

HEDDA. Yes – the manuscript?

MRS ELVSTED. Where is it?

LOEVBORG. Oh, Thea, please don't ask me that!

MRS ELVSTED. Yes, yes – I must know. I've a right to know. Now!

LOEVBORG. The manuscript. Yes. I've torn it up.

MRS ELVSTED (*screams*). No, no!

HEDDA (*involuntarily*). But that's not – !

LOEVBORG (*looks at her*). Not true, you think.

HEDDA (*controls herself*). Why – yes, of course it is, if you say so. It sounded so incredible –

LOEVBORG. It's true, nevertheless.

MRS ELVSTED. Oh, my God, my God, Hedda – he's destroyed his own book!

LOEVBORG. I have destroyed my life. Why not my life's work, too?

MRS ELVSTED. And you – did this last night?

LOEVBORG. Yes, Thea. I tore it into a thousand pieces. And scattered them out across the fjord. It's good, clean, salt water. Let it carry them away; let them drift in the current and the wind. And in a little while, they will sink. Deeper and deeper. As I shall, Thea.

MRS ELVSTED. Do you know, Eilert – this book – all my life I shall feel as though you'd killed a little child?

LOEVBORG. You're right. It is like killing a child.

MRS ELVSTED. But how could you? It was my child, too!

HEDDA (*almost inaudibly*). Oh – the child – !

MRS ELVSTED (*breathes heavily*). It's all over, then. Well – I'll go now, Hedda.

HEDDA. You're not leaving town?

MRS ELVSTED. I don't know what I'm going to do. I can't see anything except – darkness.

She goes out through the hall.

HEDDA (*waits a moment*). Aren't you going to escort her home, Mr Loevborg?

LOEVBORG. I? Through the streets? Do you want me to let
people see her with me?

HEDDA. Of course, I don't know what else may have happened
last night. But is it so utterly beyond redress?

LOEVBORG. It isn't just last night. It'll go on happening. I
know it. But the curse of it is, I don't want to live that kind
of life. I don't want to start all that again. She's broken my
courage. I can't spit in the eyes of the world any longer.

HEDDA (*as though to herself*). That pretty little fool's been
trying to shape a man's destiny. (*Looks at him.*) But how
could you be so heartless towards her?

LOEVBORG. Don't call me heartless!

HEDDA. To go and destroy the one thing that's made her life
worth living? You don't call that heartless?

LOEVBORG. Do you want to know the truth, Hedda?

HEDDA. The truth?

LOEVBORG. Promise me first – give me your word – that you'll
never let Thea know about this.

HEDDA. I give you my word.

LOEVBORG. Good. Well; what I told her just now was a lie.

HEDDA. About the manuscript?

LOEVBORG. Yes. I didn't tear it up. Or throw it in the fjord.

HEDDA. You didn't? But where is it, then?

LOEVBORG. I destroyed it, all the same. I destroyed it, Hedda!

HEDDA. I don't understand.

LOEVBORG. Thea said that what I had done was like killing a
child.

HEDDA. Yes. That's what she said.

LOEVBORG. But to kill a child isn't the worst thing a father can
do to it.

HEDDA. What could be worse than that?

LOEVBORG. Hedda – suppose a man came home one morning,
after a night of debauchery, and said to the mother of his
child: 'Look here. I've been wandering round all night.
I've been to – such-and-such a place and such-and-such a

place. And I had our child with me. I took him to – these
places. And I've lost him. Just – lost him. God knows
where he is or whose hands he's fallen into.'

HEDDA. I see. But when all's said and done, this was only a
book –

LOEVBORG. Thea's heart and soul were in that book. It was her
whole life.

HEDDA. Yes, I understand.

LOEVBORG. Well, then you must also understand that she and
I cannot possibly ever see each other again.

HEDDA. Where will you go?

LOEVBORG. Nowhere. I just want to put an end to it all. As
soon as possible.

HEDDA (*takes a step towards him*). Eilert Loevborg, listen to
me. Do it – beautifully!

LOEVBORG. Beautifully? (*Smiles.*) With a crown of vine leaves
in my hair? The way you used to dream of me – in the old
days?

HEDDA. No. I don't believe in that crown any longer. But –
do it beautifully, all the same. Just this once. Good-bye.
You must go now. And don't come back.

LOEVBORG. Adieu, madame. Give my love to George Tesman.
(*Turns to go.*)

HEDDA. Wait. I want to give you a souvenir to take with you.

*She goes over to the writing-table, opens the drawer and the
pistol-case, and comes back to* LOEVBORG *with one of the
pistols.*

LOEVBORG (*looks at her*). This? Is this the souvenir?

HEDDA (*nods slowly*). You recognize it? You looked down its
barrel once.

LOEVBORG. You should have used it then.

HEDDA. Here! Use it now!

LOEVBORG (*puts the pistol in his breast pocket*). Thank you.

HEDDA. Do it beautifully, Eilert Loevborg. Only promise me
that!

LOEVBORG. Good-bye, Hedda Gabler.

He goes out through the hall. HEDDA *stands by the door for a
moment, listening. Then she goes over to the writing-table,
takes out the package containing the manuscript, glances
inside it, pulls some of the pages half out and looks at them.
Then she takes it to the armchair by the stove and sits down
with the package in her lap. After a moment, she opens the
door of the stove; then she opens the packet.*

HEDDA (*throws one of the pages into the stove and whispers to
herself*). I'm burning your child, Thea! You with your
beautiful, wavy hair! (*She throws a few more pages into the
stove.*) The child Eilert Loevborg gave you. (*Throws the rest
of the manuscript in.*) I'm burning it! I'm burning your
child!

Act Four

The same. It is evening. The drawing-room is in darkness. The small room is illuminated by the hanging lamp over the table. The curtains are drawn across the french windows. HEDDA, *dressed in black, is walking up and down in the darkened room. Then she goes into the small room and crosses to the left. A few chords are heard from the piano. She comes back into the drawing-room.*

BERTHA *comes through the small room from the right with a lighted lamp, which she places on the table in front of the corner sofa in the drawing-room. Her eyes are red with crying, and she has black ribbons on her cap. She goes quietly out, right.* HEDDA *goes over to the french windows, draws the curtains slightly to one side and looks out into the darkness.*

A few moments later, MISS TESMAN *enters from the hall. She is dressed in mourning, with a black hat and veil.* HEDDA *goes to meet her and holds out her hand.*

MISS TESMAN. Well, Hedda, here I am in the weeds of sorrow. My poor sister has ended her struggles at last.

HEDDA. I've already heard. Tesman sent me a card.

MISS TESMAN. Yes, he promised me he would. But I thought, no, I must go and break the news of death to Hedda myself – here, in the house of life.

HEDDA. It's very kind of you.

MISS TESMAN. Ah, Rena shouldn't have chosen a time like this to pass away. This is no moment for Hedda's house to be a place of mourning.

HEDDA *(changing the subject)*. She died peacefully, Miss Tesman?

MISS TESMAN. Oh, it was quite beautiful! The end came so

calmly. And she was so happy at being able to see George once again. And say good-bye to him. Hasn't he come home yet?

HEDDA. No. He wrote that I mustn't expect him too soon. But please sit down.

MISS TESMAN. No, thank you, Hedda dear – bless you. I'd like to. But I've so little time. I must dress her and lay her out as well as I can. She shall go to her grave looking really beautiful.

HEDDA. Can't I help with anything?

MISS TESMAN. Why, you mustn't think of such a thing! Hedda Tesman mustn't let her hands be soiled by contact with death. Or her thoughts. Not at this time.

HEDDA. One can't always control one's thoughts.

MISS TESMAN (*continues*). Ah, well, that's life. Now we must start to sew poor Rena's shroud. There'll be sewing to be done in this house, too, before long, I shouldn't wonder. But not for a shroud, praise God.

GEORGE TESMAN *enters from the hall.*

HEDDA. You've come at least! Thank heavens!

TESMAN. Are you here, Auntie Juju? With Hedda? Fancy that!

MISS TESMAN. I was just on the point of leaving, dear boy. Well, have you done everything you promised me?

TESMAN. No, I'm afraid I forgot half of it. I'll have to run over again tomorrow. My head's in a complete whirl today. I can't collect my thoughts.

MISS TESMAN. But, George dear, you mustn't take it like this.

TESMAN. Oh? Well – er – how should I?

MISS TESMAN. You must be happy in your grief. Happy for what's happened. As I am.

TESMAN. Oh, yes, yes. You're thinking of Aunt Rena.

HEDDA. It'll be lonely for you now, Miss Tesman.

MISS TESMAN. For the first few days, yes. But it won't last

long, I hope. Poor dear Rena's little room isn't going to stay empty.

TESMAN. Oh? Whom are you going to move in there? What?

MISS TESMAN. Oh, there's always some poor invalid who needs care and attention.

HEDDA. Do you really want another cross like that to bear?

MISS TESMAN. Cross! God forgive you, child. It's been no cross for me.

HEDDA. But now – if a complete stranger comes to live with you – ?

MISS TESMAN. Oh, one soon makes friends with invalids. And I need so much to have someone to live for. Like you, my dear. Well, I expect there'll soon be work in this house too for an old aunt, praise God!

HEDDA. Oh – please!

TESMAN. My word, yes! What a splendid time the three of us could have together if –

HEDDA. If?

TESMAN (*uneasily*). Oh, never mind. It'll all work out. Let's hope so – what?

MISS TESMAN. Yes, yes. Well, I'm sure you two would like to be alone. (*Smiles.*) Perhaps Hedda may have something to tell you, George. Good-bye. I must go home to Rena. (*Turns to the door.*) Dear God, how strange! Now Rena is with me and with poor dear Joachim.

TESMAN. Why, yes, Auntie Juju! What?

MISS TESMAN *goes out through the hall.*

HEDDA (*follows* TESMAN *coldly and searchingly with her eyes*). I really believe this death distresses you more than it does her.

TESMAN. Oh, it isn't just Auntie Rena. It's Eilert I'm so worried about.

HEDDA (*quickly*). Is there any news of him?

TESMAN. I ran over to see him this afternoon. I wanted to tell him his manuscript was in safe hands.

HEDDA. Oh? You didn't find him?

TESMAN. No. He wasn't at home. But later I met Mrs Elvsted and she told me he'd been here early this morning.

HEDDA. Yes, just after you'd left.

TESMAN. It seems he said he'd torn the manuscript up. What?

HEDDA. Yes, he claimed to have done so.

TESMAN. You told him we had it, of course?

HEDDA. No. (*Quickly.*) Did you tell Mrs Elvsted?

TESMAN. No, I didn't like to. But you ought to have told him. Think if he should go home and do something desperate! Give me the manuscript, Hedda. I'll run over to him with it right away. Where did you put it?

HEDDA (*cold and motionless, leaning against the armchair*). I haven't got it any longer.

TESMAN. Haven't got it? What on earth do you mean?

HEDDA. I've burned it.

TESMAN (*starts, terrified*). Burned it! Burned Eilert's manuscript.

HEDDA. Don't shout. The servant will hear you.

TESMAN. Burned it! But in heaven's name – ! Oh, no, no, no! This is impossible!

HEDDA. Well, it's true.

TESMAN. But, Hedda, do you realize what you've done? That's appropriating lost property! It's against the law! By God! You ask Judge Brack and see if I'm not right.

HEDDA. You'd be well advised not to talk about it to Judge Brack or anyone else.

TESMAN. But how could you go and do such a dreadul thing? What on earth put the idea into your head? What came over you? Answer me! What?

HEDDA (*represses an almost imperceptible smile*). I did it for your sake, George.

TESMAN. For my sake?

HEDDA. When you came home this morning and described how he'd read his book to you –

TESMAN. Yes, yes?

HEDDA. You admitted you were jealous of him.

TESMAN. But, good heavens, I didn't mean it literally!

HEDDA. No matter. I couldn't bear the thought that anyone else should push you into the background.

TESMAN (*torn between doubt and joy*). Hedda – is this true? But – but – but I never realized you loved me like that! Fancy that!

HEDDA. Well, I suppose you'd better know. I'm going to have – (*Breaks off and says violently.*) No, no – you'd better ask your Auntie Juju. She'll tell you.

TESMAN. Hedda! I think I understand what you mean. (*Clasps his hands.*) Good heavens, can it really be true? What?

HEDDA. Don't shout. The servant will hear you.

TESMAN (*laughing with joy*). The servant! I say, that's good! The servant! Why, that's Bertha! I'll run out and tell her at once!

HEDDA (*clenches her hands in despair*). Oh, it's destroying me, all this – it's destroying me!

TESMAN. I say, Hedda, what's up? What?

HEDDA (*cold, controlled*). Oh, it's all so – absurd – George.

TESMAN. Absurd? That I'm so happy? But surely – ? Ah, well – perhaps I won't say anything to Bertha.

HEDDA. No, do. She might as well know, too.

TESMAN. No, no, I won't tell her yet. But Auntie Juju – I must let her know! And you – you called me George! For the first time! Fancy that! Oh, it'll make Auntie Juju so happy, all this! So very happy!

HEDDA. Will she be happy when she heard I've burned Eilert Loevborg's manuscript – for your sake?

TESMAN. No, I'd forgotten about that. Of course, no one must be allowed to know about the manuscript. But that you're burning with love for me, Hedda, I must certainly let Auntie Juju know that. I say, I wonder if young wives often feel like that towards their husbands? What?

HEDDA. You might ask Auntie Juju about that, too.

TESMAN. I will, as soon as I get the chance. (*Looks uneasy and thoughtful again.*) But I say, you know, that manuscript. Dreadful business. Poor Eilert!

MRS ELVSTED, *dressed as on her first visit, with hat and overcoat, enters from the hall.*

MRS ELVSTED (*greets them hastily and tremulously*). Oh, Hedda dear, do please forgive me for coming here again.

HEDDA. Why, Thea, what's happened?

TESMAN. Is it anything to do with Eilert Loevborg? What?

MRS ELVSTED. Yes – I'm so dreadfully afraid he may have met with an accident.

HEDDA (*grips her arm*). You think so?

TESMAN. But, good heavens, Mrs Elvsted, what makes you think that?

MRS ELVSTED. I heard them talking about him at the boarding-house, as I went in. Oh, there are the most terrible rumours being spread about him in town today.

TESMAN. Er – yes, I heard about them, too. But I can testify that he went straight home to bed. Fancy –!

HEDDA. Well – what did they say in the boarding-house?

MRS ELVSTED. Oh, I couldn't find out anything. Either they didn't know, or else – They stopped talking when they saw me. And I didn't dare to ask.

TESMAN (*fidgets uneasily*). We must hope – we must hope you misheard them, Mrs Elvsted.

MRS ELVSTED. No, no, I'm sure it was him they were talking about. I heard them say something about a hospital –

TESMAN. Hospital!

HEDDA. Oh no, surely that's impossible!

MRS ELVSTED. Oh, I became so afraid. So I went up to his rooms and asked to see him.

HEDDA. Do you think that was wise, Thea?

MRS ELVSTED. Well, what else could I do? I couldn't bear the uncertainty any longer.

TESMAN. But *you* didn't manage to find him either? What?

MRS ELVSTED. No. And they had no idea where he was. They said he hadn't been home since yesterday afternoon.

TESMAN. Since yesterday? Fancy that!

MRS ELVSTED. I'm sure he must have met with an accident.

TESMAN. Hedda, I wonder if I ought to go into town and make one or two enquiries?

HEDDA. No, no, don't you get mixed up in this.

> JUDGE BRACK *enters from the hall, hat in hand.* BERTHA, *who has opened the door for him, closes it. He looks serious and greets them silently.*

TESMAN. Hullo, my dear Judge. Fancy seeing you!

BRACK. I had to come and talk to you.

TESMAN. I can see Auntie Juju's told you the news.

BRACK. Yes, I've heard about that, too.

TESMAN. Tragic, isn't it?

BRACK. Well, my dear chap, that depends how you look at it.

TESMAN (*looks uncertainly at him*). Has something else happened?

BRACK. Yes.

HEDDA. Another tragedy?

BRACK. That also depends on how you look at it, Mrs Tesman.

MRS ELVSTED. Oh, it's something to do with Eilert Loevborg!

BRACK (*looks at her for a moment*). How did you guess? Perhaps you've heard already – ?

MRS ELVSTED (*confused*). No, no, not at all – I –

TESMAN. For heaven's sake, tell us!

BRACK (*shrugs his shoulders*). Well, I'm afraid they've taken him to the hospital. He's dying.

MRS ELVSTED (*screams*). Oh God, God!

TESMAN. The hospital! Dying!

HEDDA (*involuntarily*). So quickly!

MRS ELVSTED (*weeping*). Oh, Hedda! And we parted enemies!

HEDDA (*whispers*). Thea – Thea!

MRS ELVSTED (*ignoring her*). I must see him! I must see him before he dies!

BRACK. It's no use, Mrs Elvsted. No one's allowed to see him now.

MRS ELVSTED. But what's happened to him? You must tell me!

TESMAN. He hasn't tried to do anything to himself? What?

HEDDA. Yes, he has. I'm sure of it.

TESMAN. Hedda, how can you – ?

BRACK (*who has not taken his eyes from her*). I'm afraid you've guessed correctly, Mrs Tesman.

MRS ELVSTED. How dreadful!

TESMAN. Attempted suicide! Fancy that!

HEDDA. Shot himself!

BRACK. Right again, Mrs Tesman.

MRS ELVSTED (*tries to compose herself*). When did this happen, Judge Brack?

BRACK. This afternoon. Between three and four.

TESMAN. But, good heavens – where? What?

BRACK (*a little hesitantly*). Where? Why, my dear chap, in his rooms, of course.

MRS ELVSTED. No, that's impossible. I was there soon after six.

BRACK. Well, it must have been somewhere else, then. I don't know exactly. I only know that they found him. He's shot himself – through the breast.

MRS ELVSTED. Oh, how horrible! That he should end like that!

HEDDA (*to* BRACK). Through the breast, you said?

BRACK. That is what I said.

HEDDA. Not through the head?

BRACK. Through the breast, Mrs Tesman.

HEDDA. The breast. Yes; yes. That's good, too.

BRACK. Why, Mrs Tesman?

HEDDA. Oh – no, I didn't mean anything.

TESMAN. And the wound's dangerous, you say? What?

BRACK. Mortal. He's probably already dead.

MRS ELVSTED. Yes, yes – I feel it! It's all over. All over. Oh
Hedda – !

TESMAN. But, tell me, how did you manage to learn all this?

BRACK (*curtly*). From the police. I spoke to one of them.

HEDDA (*loudly, clearly*). Thank God! At last!

TESMAN (*appalled*). For God's sake, Hedda, what are you
saying?

HEDDA. I am saying there's beauty in what he has done.

BRACK. Hm – Mrs Tesman –

TESMAN. Beauty! Oh, but I say!

MRS ELVSTED. Hedda, how can you talk of beauty in con-
nexion with a thing like this?

HEDDA. Eilert Loevborg has settled his account with life. He's
had the courage to do what – what he had to do.

MRS ELVSTED. No, that's not why it happened. He did it
because he was mad.

TESMAN. He did it because he was desperate.

HEDDA. You're wrong! I know!

MRS ELVSTED. He must have been mad. The same as when he
tore up the manuscript.

BRACK (*starts*). Manuscript? Did he tear it up?

MRS ELVSTED. Yes. Last night.

TESMAN (*whispers*). Oh, Hedda, we shall never be able to
escape from this.

BRACK. Hm. Strange.

TESMAN (*wanders round the room*). To think of Eilert dying
like that. And not leaving behind him the thing that would
have made his name endure.

MRS ELVSTED. If only it could be pieced together again!

TESMAN. Yes, yes, yes! If only it could! I'd give anything –

MRS ELVSTED. Perhaps it can, Mr Tesman.

TESMAN. What do you mean?

MRS ELVSTED (*searches in the pocket of her dress*). Look. I kept the notes he dictated it from.

HEDDA (*takes a step nearer*). Ah!

TESMAN. You kept them, Mrs Elvsted! What?

MRS ELVSTED. Yes, here they are. I brought them with me when I left home. They've been in my pocket ever since.

TESMAN. Let me have a look.

MRS ELVSTED (*hands him a wad of small sheets of paper*). They're in a terrible muddle. All mixed up.

TESMAN. I say, just fancy if we could sort them out! Perhaps if we work on them together – ?

MRS ELVSTED. Oh, yes! Let's try, anyway!

TESMAN. We'll manage it. We must! I shall dedicate my life to this.

HEDDA. *You*, George? Your life?

TESMAN. Yes – well, all the time I can spare. My book'll have to wait. Hedda, you do understand? What? I owe it to Eilert's memory.

HEDDA. Perhaps.

TESMAN. Well, my dear Mrs Elvsted, you and I'll have to pool our brains. No use crying over spilt milk, what? We must try to approach this matter calmly.

MRS ELVSTED. Yes, yes, Mr Tesman. I'll do my best.

TESMAN. Well, come over here and let's start looking at these notes right away. Where shall we sit? Here? No, the other room. You'll excuse us, won't you, Judge? Come along with me, Mrs Elvsted.

MRS ELVSTED. Oh, God! If only we can manage to do it!

TESMAN *and* MRS ELVSTED *go into the rear room. He takes off his hat and overcoat. They sit at the table beneath the hanging lamp and absorb themselves in the notes.* HEDDA *walks across to the stove and sits in the armchair. After a moment,* BRACK *goes over to her.*

HEDDA (*half aloud*). Oh, Judge! This act of Eilert Loevborg's
– doesn't it give one a sense of release!

BRACK. Release, Mrs Hedda? Well, it's a release for him, of
course –

HEDDA. Oh, I don't mean him – I mean me! The release of
knowing that someone can do something really brave! Something beautiful!

BRACK (*smiles*). Hm – my dear Mrs Hedda –

HEDDA. Oh, I know what you're going to say. You're a
bourgeois at heart, too, just like – ah, well!

BRACK (*looks at her*). Eilert Loevborg has meant more to you
than you're willing to admit to yourself. Or am I wrong?

HEDDA. I'm not answering questions like that from you. I only
know that Eilert Loevborg has had the courage to live
according to his own principles. And now, at last, he's done
something big! Something beautiful! To have the courage
and the will to rise from the feast of life so early!

BRACK. It distresses me deeply, Mrs Hedda, but I'm afraid I
must rob you of that charming illusion.

HEDDA. Illusion?

BRACK. You wouldn't have been allowed to keep it for long,
anyway.

HEDDA. What do you mean?

BRACK. He didn't shoot himself on purpose.

HEDDA. Not on purpose?

BRACK. No. It didn't happen quite the way I told you.

HEDDA. Have you been hiding something? What is it?

BRACK. In order to spare poor Mrs Elvsted's feelings, I per-
mitted myself one or two small – equivocations.

HEDDA. What?

BRACK. To begin with, he is already dead.

HEDDA. He died at the hospital?

BRACK. Yes. Without regaining consciousness.

HEDDA. What else haven't you told us?

BRACK. The incident didn't take place at his lodgings.

HEDDA. Well, that's utterly unimportant.

BRACK. Not utterly. The fact is, you see, that Eilert Loevborg was found shot in Mademoiselle Danielle's boudoir.

HEDDA (*almost jumps up, but instead sinks back in her chair*). That's impossible. He can't have been there today.

BRACK. He was there this afternoon. He went to ask for something he claimed they'd taken from him. Talked of some crazy nonsense about a child which had got lost –

HEDDA. Oh! So that was the reason!

BRACK. I thought at first he might have been referring to his manuscript. But I hear he destroyed that himself. So he must have meant his pocket-book – I suppose.

HEDDA. Yes, I suppose so. So they found him there?

BRACK. Yes; there. With a discharged pistol in his breast pocket. The shot had wounded him mortally.

HEDDA. Yes. In the breast.

BRACK. No. In the – stomach. The – lower part –

HEDDA (*looks at him with an expression of repulsion*). That, too! Oh, why does everything I touch become mean and ludicrous? It's like a curse!

BRACK. There's something else, Mrs Hedda. It's rather disagreeable, too.

HEDDA. What?

BRACK. The pistol he had on him –

HEDDA. Yes? What about it?

BRACK. He must have stolen it.

HEDDA (*jumps up*). Stolen it! That isn't true! He didn't!

BRACK. It's the only explanation. He must have stolen it. Ssh!

TESMAN *and* MRS ELVSTED *have got up from the table in the rear room and come into the drawing-room.*

TESMAN (*his hands full of papers*). Hedda, I can't see properly under that lamp. Do you think – ?

HEDDA. I am thinking.

TESMAN. Do you think we could possibly use your writing-table for a little? What?

HEDDA. Yes, of course. (*Quickly.*) No, wait! Let me tidy it up first.

TESMAN. Oh, don't you trouble about that. There's plenty of room.

HEDDA. No, no, let me tidy it up first, I say. I'll take these in and put them on the piano. Here.

She pulls an object, covered with sheets of music, out from under the bookcase, puts some more sheets on top and carries it all into the rear room and away to the left. TESMAN *puts his papers on the writing-table and moves the lamp over from the corner table. He and* MRS ELVSTED *sit down and begin working again.* HEDDA *comes back.*

(*Behind* MRS ELVSTED'S *chair, ruffles her hair gently.*) Well, my pretty Thea. And how is work progressing on Eilert Loevborg's memorial?

MRS ELVSTED (*looks up at her, dejectedly*). Oh, it's going to be terribly difficult to get these into any order.

TESMAN. We've got to do it. We must! After all, putting other people's papers into order is rather my speciality, what?

HEDDA *goes over to the stove and sits on one of the footstools.* BRACK *stands over her, leaning against the armchair.*

HEDDA (*whispers*). What was that you were saying about the pistol?

BRACK (*softly*). I said he must have stolen it.

HEDDA. Why do you think that?

BRACK. Because any other explanation is unthinkable, Mrs Hedda. Or ought to be.

HEDDA. I see.

BRACK (*looks at her for a moment*). Eilert Loevborg was here this morning. Wasn't he?

HEDDA. Yes.

BRACK. Were you alone with him?

HEDDA. For a few moments.

BRACK. You didn't leave the room while he was here?

HEDDA. No.

BRACK. Think again. Are you sure you didn't go out for a moment?

HEDDA. Oh – yes, I might have gone into the hall. Just for a few seconds.

BRACK. And where was your pistol-case during this time?

HEDDA. I'd locked it in that –

BRACK. Er – Mrs Hedda?

HEDDA. It was lying over there on my writing-table.

BRACK. Have you looked to see if both the pistols are still there?

HEDDA. No.

BRACK. You needn't bother. I saw the pistol Loevborg had when they found him. I recognized it at once. From yesterday. And other occasions.

HEDDA. Have you got it?

BRACK. No. The police have it.

HEDDA. What will the police do with this pistol?

BRACK. Try to trace the owner.

HEDDA. Do you think they'll succeed?

BRACK (*leans down and whispers*). No, Hedda Gabler. Not as long as I hold my tongue.

HEDDA (*looks nervously at him*). And if you don't?

BRACK (*shrugs his shoulders*). You could always say he'd stolen it.

HEDDA. I'd rather die!

BRACK (*smiles*). People say that. They never do it.

HEDDA (*not replying*). And suppose the pistol wasn't stolen? And they trace the owner? What then?

BRACK. There'll be a scandal, Hedda.

HEDDA. A scandal!

BRACK. Yes, a scandal. The thing you're so frightened of. You'll have to appear in court together with Mademoiseell

Danielle. She'll have to explain how it all happened. Was it
an accident, or was it – homicide? Was he about to take the
pistol from his pocket to threaten her? And did it go off?
Or did she snatch the pistol from his hand, shoot him and
then put it back in his pocket? She might quite easily have
done it. She's a resourceful lady, is Mademoiselle Danielle.

HEDDA. But I have nothing to do with this repulsive business.

BRACK. No. But you'll have to answer one question. Why did
you give Eilert Loevborg this pistol? And what conclusions
will people draw when it is proved you did give it to him?

HEDDA (*bow her head*). That's true. I hadn't thought of that.

BRACK. Well, luckily there's no danger as long as I hold my
tongue.

HEDDA. (*looks up at him*). In other words, I'm in your power,
Judge. From now on, you've got your hold over me.

BRACK (*whispers, more slowly*). Hedda, my dearest – believe
me – I will not abuse my position.

HEDDA. Nevertheless, I'm in your power. Dependent on your
will, and your demands. Not free. Still not free! (*Rises
passionately.*) No. I couldn't bear that. No.

BRACK (*looks half-derisively at her*). Most people resign themselves to the inevitable, sooner or later.

HEDDA (*returns his gaze*). Possibly they do.

She goes across to the writing-table.

(*Represses an involuntary smile and says in* TESMAN'S *voice*.)
Well, George. Think you'll be able to manage? What?

TESMAN. Heaven knows, dear. This is going to take months
and months.

HEDDA (*in the same tone as before*). Fancy that, by Jove! (*Runs
her hands gently through* MRS ELVSTED'S *hair*.) Doesn't it
feel strange, Thea? Here you are working away with Tesman
just the way you used to work with Eilert Loevborg.

MRS ELVSTED. Oh – if only I can inspire your husband, too!

HEDDA. Oh, it'll come. In time.

TESMAN. Yes – do you know, Hedda, I really think I'm beginning to feel a bit – well – that way. But you go back and talk to Judge Brack.

HEDDA. Can't I be of use to you two in any way?

TESMAN. No, none at all. (*Turns his head.*) You'll have to keep Hedda company from now on, Judge, and see she doesn't get bored. If you don't mind.

BRACK (*glances at* HEDDA). It'll be a pleasure.

HEDDA. Thank you. But I'm tired this evening. I think I'll lie down on the sofa in there for a little while.

TESMAN. Yes, dear – do. What?

> HEDDA *goes into the rear room and draws the curtains behind her. Short pause. Suddenly she begins to play a frenzied dance melody on the piano.*

MRS ELVSTED (*starts up from her chair*). Oh, what's that?

TESMAN (*runs to the doorway*). Hedda dear, please! Don't play dance music tonight! Think of Auntie Rena. And Eilert.

HEDDA (*puts her head through the curtains*). And Auntie Juju. And all the rest of them. From now on I'll be quiet.

> *She closes the curtains behind her.*

TESMAN (*at the writing-table*). It distresses her to watch us doing this. I say, Mrs Elvsted, I've an idea. Why don't you move in with Auntie Juju? I'll run over each evening, and we can sit and work there. What?

MRS ELVSTED. Yes, that might be the best plan.

HEDDA (*from the rear room*). I can hear what you're saying, Tesman. But how shall I spend the evenings out here?

TESMAN (*looking through his papers*). Oh, I'm sure Judge Brack'll be kind enough to come over and keep you company. You won't mind my not being here, Judge?

BRACK (*in the armchair, calls gaily*). I'll be delighted, Mrs Tesman. I'll be here every evening. We'll have great fun together, you and I.

HEDDA (*loud and clear*). Yes, that'll suit you, won't it, Judge? The only cock on the dunghill –

A shot is heard from the rear room. TESMAN, MRS ELVSTED *and* JUDGE BRACK *start from their chairs.*

TESMAN. Oh, she's playing with those pistols again.

He pulls the curtains aside and runs in. MRS ELVSTED *follows him.* HEDDA *is lying dead on the sofa. Confusion and shouting.* BERTHA *enters in alarm from the right.*

TESMAN (*screams to* BRACK). She's shot herself! Shot herself in the head! Fancy that!

BRACK (*half paralysed in the armchair*). But, good God! People don't do such things!

Note on the Translation

The main problem in translating *Hedda Gabler* is to contrast the snobbish and consciously upper-class speech of Hedda and Judge Brack with the naïve and homely way of talking shared by Miss Tesman, Bertha and George Tesman. Hedda is a General's daughter and lets no one forget it. George Tesman has unconsciously acquired the nanny-like mode of speech of the old aunts who brought him up. He addresses Aunt Juliana as *Tante Julle*, a particularly irritating and baby-like abbreviation which drives Hedda mad every time he uses it. The last straw is when he asks her to address the old lady by it, too. To render this as Auntie Julie, as has usually been done, is completely to miss the point; it must be a ridiculous nickname such as Juju. When Brack tells Hedda where Loevborg has shot himself, he must make it clear to her that the bullet destroyed his sexual organs; otherwise Hedda's reactions make no sense. To translate this as 'belly' or 'bowels' is again to miss the point, yet Brack must not use the phrase 'sexual organs' directly; he is far too subtle a campaigner to speak so bluntly to a lady. What he says is: 'In the – stomach. The – lower part.' I have altered the name of the red-haired singer from Mademoiselle Diana, which is difficult to say in English and has an improbable ring about it, to Mademoiselle Danielle.

In the Norwegian, Hedda addresses her husband as Tesman except on the crucial occasions at the end of Act 1 and in Act 4, when she deliberately switches to his Christian name. Similarly, Brack calls Hedda Mrs Tesman when anyone else is present, but Mrs Hedda when they are alone together; only towards the very end of the play does he address her simply as Hedda. Although this usage is un-English, even for the period, it is, in fact, effective on the stage when one has the illusion of eavesdropping on a foreign nineteenth-century family, and I have let it stand. To allow Brack to call her Hedda the first time we see them alone together in Act 2 suggests an intimacy which they have not yet reached.

M.M.

Methuen's Modern Plays

EDITED BY JOHN CULLEN AND GEOFFREY STRACHAN

Paul Ableman	*Green Julia*
Jean Anouilh	*Antigone*
	Becket
	Poor Bitos
	Ring Round the Moon
	The Lark
	The Rehearsal
	The Fighting Cock
	Dear Antoine
	The Director of the Opera
John Arden	*Serjeant Musgrave's Dance*
	The Workhouse Donkey
	Armstrong's Last Goodnight
	Left-Handed Liberty
	Soldier, Soldier and other plays
	Two Autobiographical Plays
John Arden and	*The Business of Good Government*
Margaretta D'Arcy	*The Royal Pardon*
	The Hero Rises up
	The Island of the Mighty
Ayckbourn, Bowen	*Mixed Doubles*
Brook, Campton	
Melly, Owen, Pinter,	
Saunders, Weldon	
Brendan Behan	*The Quare Fellow*
	The Hostage
	Richard's Cork Leg
Barry Bermange	*No Quarter and the Interview*